T0300277

ROUTLEDGE LIBRARY EDITIONS:
SOVIET POLITICS

Volume 17

SOVIET RUSSIA

SOVIET RUSSIA

An Introduction

JACOB MILLER

Routledge
Taylor & Francis Group

LONDON AND NEW YORK

First published in 1955 by Hutchinson & Co. (Publishers) Ltd.

This edition first published in 2024
by Routledge
4 Park Square, Milton Park, Abingdon, Oxon OX14 4RN

and by Routledge
605 Third Avenue, New York, NY 10158

Routledge is an imprint of the Taylor & Francis Group, an informa business

© 1955 Hutchinson & Co. (Publishers) Ltd.

British Library Cataloguing in Publication Data
A catalogue record for this book is available from the British Library

ISBN: 978-1-032-67165-9 (Set)
ISBN: 978-1-032-67477-3 (Volume 17) (hbk)
ISBN: 978-1-032-67482-7 (Volume 17) (pbk)
ISBN: 978-1-032-67479-7 (Volume 17) (ebk)

DOI: 10.4324/9781032674797

Publisher's Note
The publisher has gone to great lengths to ensure the quality of this reprint but points out that some imperfections in the original copies may be apparent.

Disclaimer
The publisher has made every effort to trace copyright holders and would welcome correspondence from those they have been unable to trace.

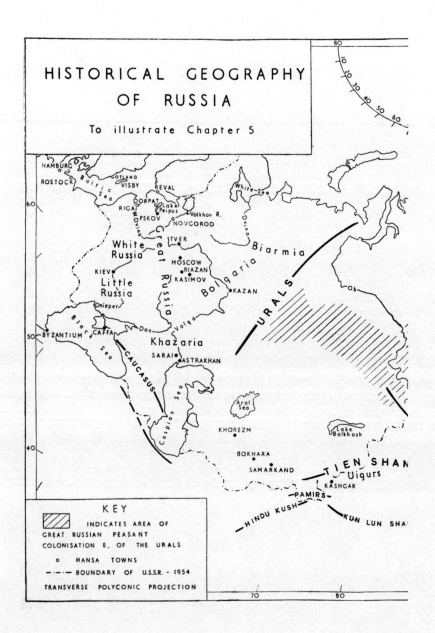

HISTORICAL GEOGRAPHY
OF RUSSIA

To illustrate Chapter 5

KEY

INDICATES AREA OF
GREAT RUSSIAN PEASANT
COLONISATION E. OF THE URALS

o   HANSA TOWNS

—·—·— BOUNDARY OF U.S.S.R. - 1954

TRANSVERSE POLYCONIC PROJECTION

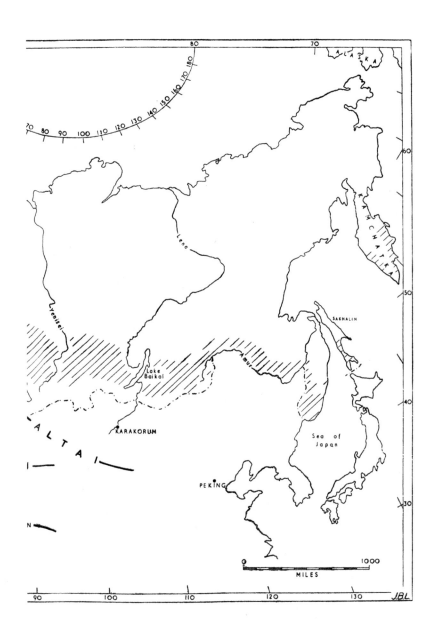

80   70

180 170 160 150 140 130 120 110 100 90 80 70

A L A S K A

60

K A M C H A T K A

Lena

50

Yenisei

SAKHALIN

Amur

Lake Baikal

40

A L T A I

KARAKORUM

Sea of Japan

PEKING

30

N

1000

MILES

90   100   110   120   130

JBL

SOVIET RUSSIA

An Introduction

by

JACOB MILLER, M.A.

LECTURER IN SOVIET SOCIAL AND ECONOMIC INSTITUTIONS,
UNIVERSITY OF GLASGOW, JOINT EDITOR OF *Soviet Studies*

HUTCHINSON'S UNIVERSITY LIBRARY
Hutchinson House, London, W. 1

Hutchinson & Co. (Publishers) Ltd.

London   Melbourne   Sydney
Auckland   Bombay   Cape Town
New York   Toronto

First Published · 1955

Printed in Great Britain by
WILLIAM BRENDON AND SON LTD
THE MAYFLOWER PRESS
(late of Plymouth)
WATFORD

CONTENTS

CONTENTS

PREFATORY NOTE

THE footnotes in this book (except the one on p. 86) have been added in October 1954 to indicate the principal developments in Russia since the book was completed early in that year. All these developments are a spreading and deepening of the great changes of 1952–53. These changes are dealt with in the text only within the general purpose of the book, which is to lay out the chief factors in Russian history (both remote and recent) which have made the Russian peoples what they are, and to say how they manage their affairs. A fuller account of their organisation and ideas and of the transition which they made in 1952–53, and how they are handling this transition and its consequences, requires a separate book.

Following English usage, the name Russia is used throughout for the U.S.S.R.; the Great-Russian people (the Russian people proper) are always called Great-Russians, and the Little Russians (Ukrainians) and White-Russians (Byelorussians) are also called by their proper names. The Black-Russians mentioned on p. 176 ceased to exist in the middle ages.

Similarly, the name of the Tartars and of their empire, Tartary, are spelled according to English usage: the more learned spelling is Tatars for the people—and there is no learned spelling for Tartary.

J. M.

CHAPTER I

PERIODS AND PEOPLE

So much has happened in Russia since the Bolshevik Revolution of November 1917 that the first need is to set it in some sort of order, to divide the history into periods. It is not a good idea to use people for these periods in the way we use our kings and queens, because too much has happened in a single lifetime, or, in other cases, life has been too short. For instance, the list of Presidents of the U.S.S.R. is:

1917–19   Sverdlov, son of a Jewish master-craftsman, was a political organizer who had spent most of his adult life in prison and exile, and who died at the age of thirty-three in the great European influenza epidemic of 1918–19;

1919–46   Kalinin, a Leningrad metal-worker of Russian peasant stock, was selected to represent, in the public eye, the peasant interest in the new state; his presidency covers the civil wars, the "new economic policy", industrialization and collectivization and the Second World War;

1946–53   Shvernik, a Leningrad worker of working-class stock; head of the trade union movement;

1953–   Voroshilov, Ukrainian son of a regular soldier; served his time as mechanic; Marshal of the Red Army; represents the generation of the 1905 and 1917 revolutions in a government now mostly composed of men of the next generation.

So we could not speak of the Sverdlov period, because Sverdlov died too soon; while we cannot speak of the Kalinin period, because his presidency covered a number of periods.

When the Russians write about their own modern history, they recognize three main periods, and their names for them are "the transition from capitalism to socialism" 1917–36; the period of "the building of socialism" 1936–52; and the

9

period of "the completing of socialism" 1952 onwards. By this they mean that the first nineteen years after the revolution were occupied by all kinds of preparatory work—civil wars, party disputes, building factories and towns, reorganizing farming—which had to be done *before* socialism in their sense of the word could be introduced, and all this was only laying the foundations for socialism. The next sixteen years were occupied in building the house of socialism, fighting the war and rebuilding the wrecked house; by 1952 this was finished and the furnishing of the house was started.

Or, when they look at their history another way, the Russians write of a few years at a time and name them after the nation's work in that period. Then 1917–18 is the time of the political revolution; 1918–21 is the period of the civil war and "war communism"; 1921–29 is the period of the "new economic policy" when private enterprise was encouraged so that production was restored ready for the beginning of planning; 1929–32 is the great agony, the physical crisis of industrialization and collectivization in the first five-year plan; 1933–41 is the time of the long upward haul from the turning point made by that physical crisis, continually over-shadowed by the coming war; 1941–45 is the war; 1946–48 is rehabilitation; 1948–52 is the completion of industrializa-tion; and 1953 is the year of change from building the house of socialism to starting to live in it.

If this is how Russian history looks from the inside, we all know that it looks very different from the outside. Neither of these views is wholly untrue; but for the most part what looks important outside Russia may just be the goings on of politicians when looked at from the inside; and what is really important inside may be just puzzling or not noticed at all from the outside.

What this book tries to do is to say in broad outline what the Russian people have done and how it looks to them—remembering that the Russian people for the most part are not politicians, but use the politicians that lie to hand for doing the jobs that need to be done, just as we do. When the jobs mean that one man or a few have to be given a lot of power, the Russians naturally give them the power, and take it back again when the job is done: and they leave it to their writers and journalists (and ours) to argue about whether this is "democratic" or not. This book will not bother with arguments like this, because they are only propaganda and get nobody anywhere.

It looks to the Russian people at present that they have succeeded in building the house of socialism, and are beginning to settle themselves down to living in it. So we shall call the years 1917–52 the period of Early Soviet Socialism, and the period beginning in 1954 the period of Middle Soviet Socialism: the year in between, 1953, is the year of the great change or the revolution out of Early into Middle Soviet Socialism. The Early period is conveniently divided into three sub-periods:

1917–36 laying the foundations;
1936–41 building the house;
1941–52 fighting for the house, rebuilding it, and finishing the building.

Because the politicians were given a great deal of power during Early Soviet Socialism, their names are important. Here are the lists of the people who have held the key jobs since the revolution of 1917, except for the Presidents, whose names are given on page 9:

Prime Ministers
1917–24   Lenin
1924–30   Rykov
1930–41   Molotov
1941–53   Stalin
1953–   Malenkov

Senior Secretaries of the Communist Party
1917–19   Sverdlov in general charge
1919–21   Krestinsky ⎫ under
1921–22   Molotov   ⎬ Stalin
1922–53   Stalin   ⎭
1953–   Khrushchov

Chiefs of the Political Police

1917–26	Dzerzhinsky
1926–34	Menzhinsky
1934–36	Yagoda
1936–38	Yezhov
1938–53	Beria
1953–	Kruglov

Foreign Ministers

1917–18	Trotsky
1918–30	Chicherin
1930–39	Litvinov
1939–49	Molotov
1949–53	Vishinsky
1953–	Molotov

War Ministers

1917–18	none
1918–24	Trotsky
1924–25	Frunze
1925–41	Voroshilov
1941–46	Stalin
1946–	Bulganin

Heads of Trade Unions' Central Council

1917–18	Zinoviev
1918–29	Tomsky
1930–46	Shvernik
1946–53	Kuznetsov
1953–	Shvernik

The Communist International

1919–26	Zinoviev (President)
1926–29	Bukharin (President)
1929–35	nobody in charge (Manuilsky head of the Russian delegation)
1935–43	Dimitrov (senior secretary)
1943	abolished

CHAPTER II

INDUSTRIALIZATION

THE most obvious thing that the Russian people have done, and one which influences all their other work, is the industrialization of their country. To understand why they decided that this had to be done, and why they thought it had to be done in a way radically different from the earlier industrializations of Britain, France, U.S.A., Germany, Belgium, northern Italy and Japan, we have to look into the back history of industry in Russia.

The first real industry came to Russia in the time of Peter the Great in the early eighteenth century. It consisted mostly of war industries in state-owned factories manned by state-owned serfs, and began the Russian tradition of the state as the chief industrialist. After Peter, there was a scattered development of light industry by merchants to provide goods for trade and, to a greater extent, by the nobles using the labour of their slaves to make cloth and other goods from the raw materials of their own estates. There were no "free" workers, and the merchants bought entire villages for labour: this was stopped by the nobles in 1762, to keep the labour for themselves, but was permitted again in 1798. Thus almost all industry was run on slave and serf labour, often in very large primitive workshops without wages or machinery, though there was a strong pressure of economic circumstances towards wage labour. The only heavy industry until the middle of the nineteenth century, the iron-smelting in the Urals, was manned by labour which was bought and sold with the furnaces, but by this time a new kind of manufacturing was coming in, which had to use steam power and free wage labour: this was the cotton textile industry, through which other countries had come to industrialize and which was coming into being in Russia in the 1840s but could not expand freely in the existing conditions. It was the Crimean War, however, that made the necessity of modern industry and transport overwhelmingly obvious. But for this, two basic elements were required—a free labour force and capital investment (the technical knowledge had already been created elsewhere and, as was already being done for the cotton industry, could be imported). So the slave peasants of the nobles and the serf peasants of the state were freed as persons in 1861, but remained taxpaying members of their native villages wherever they worked: such bondage to the village was not ended till 1906, so that it is only some fifty years since a Russian villager was really free to become a townsman.

Nevertheless, there began to be heavy industry in Russia from the 1860s onwards. The first big development was the building of railways, which of course made a great difference to the merchants. Dostoievsky in 1876 writes that a big change has come over the merchant class: a merchant's ambitions are no longer confined to the giving of dinners and balls for the local notables—the merchant has become a notable himself, and in the process has become also a speculator of the European type, gambling in the money market. Speculative foreign capital also began to find its way into Russia; and the old nobility lost their monopoly of government when the Finance Minister Witte directed the economic policy of the state in favour of industry in the 1890s. But the financial jugglery outran the amount of useful industrial development, and the whole process ended in the great slump of 1901–3. A new Russia came out of this slump: industry survived by being heavily cartelized, concentrated in big physical units, and in large measure subject to foreign capital; the disaster had brought together the scattered groups of industrial workers and made them into a working class in their own minds, so that a political party aiming to represent the working class could be formed by 1903.

The slump had a profound effect in other ways also. The Russians had long been debating the advantages of westernization and its probable cost to the Russian way of life, and had seen its coming to Russia, its creation of new virtues and strange vices. Plainly, industry was bound to come; but the question was, should it come under Tsarist rule and regulation which had a stranglehold on private enterprise and yet shared responsibility for the slump; should it come under republican private enterprise, run not by God-fearing Puritans or by Scrooges who would starve themselves as well as the Cratchits, but by the big-bellied strong-fisted bullies who were the Russian capitalists then (and are still often the cartoon figures for foreign capitalists); or should it come in a new way which, whatever its own evils, would not have these? These were the questions which Russia brought out of the slump of 1901–3, and which successive governments put to the country thereafter.

The first stage was the revolution that failed in 1905 to unseat Tsarist control and establish a capitalist state. The Tsarist government remained in power, but under Stolypin abolished the last legal ties which still bound the villager to his village. This made it easier for poor peasants to give up their land and go to the towns, so that there was greatly hastened the process of concentrating agricultural land in the hands of a rural minority who, aided by government loans, were becoming farmers in the western sense, that is, working landowners employing landless labour on their own farms. This yeoman class, which would have become the rural backbone of a capitalist Russia, were the hated originals of the kulaks, the "fists", whose traditional name was used for rather different purposes later on.

The first solution which Russia tried was therefore the growth of capitalism under Tsarist control, and it was under this system that Russia went into the First World War. As everybody knows, this was the system that sent soldiers into the trenches without even a rifle apiece; and quite apart from the scandals of the court and administration, the system could not fight, much less survive, the war.

The second solution which Russia tried was that of capitalist republicanism under Prince Lvov (and later Kerensky) in February 1917. The advantage with which this government began was that it was a step forward from Tsarism; but its disadvantages were tremendous: Russian capitalists were subservient by training and experience to the Tsarist system and to foreign banks and firms; the government did not feel sovereign and did not look masterful; at the same time, the native capitalist stood in people's minds for cruelty and self-indulgence. The February revolution, moreover, had not been intended as a changing of horses in mid-stream: the Russians wanted to get out of the war. But the new government continued it. Thirdly, as a step forward from Tsarism, the new government had the support of a multitude of feckless and well-meaning progressives who could only arouse mistrust among responsible ordinary people. And fourthly, the change had come so late in the day that the working-class leaders knew the kind of job the capitalists would have to do in industrializing Russia, and some of them convinced themselves and their supporters that they could do it better and at less cost. So the February revolution was succeeded by that of November because the leaders of the November revolution not only had the long view and knew what the country was in for, but were also prepared to take on the responsibility for running an industrialization. The Russian working class rejected its capitalists as well as its Tsarists as incompetent, so the alternative was those amongst the socialists who were prepared to do the capitalists' job of industrialization.

It cannot be too greatly emphasized that the problem of industrialization was not changed by this political revolution: all that had been decided was that two possible ways of handling the problem had been rejected. The problem remained the same: gathering together from the resources of a poor country enough concentrations of wealth to establish a large fixed heavy industrial capital (factories, mines, railways, power stations) and to feed and clothe a labour force while it was learning to be a modern skilled working class. Even rich countries have not found this problem to be one which can be solved without people going more than short, without force in getting people off the land, without savage legal sanctions (such as hanging for sheep stealing), without sending enslaved peasants to Barbadoes, without transportation to Botany Bay, without inequality and oppression, and without getting resources from outside the country. The only difference in Russia of 1917 was that, since all this was known, from European experience, the Russian working-class leaders saw no reason why the process should not be under working-class control. They did not expect it to be an easy or a kindly process; they knew that the small Russian working class would have to carry with it, by force or persuasion, the Russian peasantry and all the border nationalities within the Tsarist empire, and they made their preparations in this expectation.

As various groups came together in the making of the revolution, so also the various preparations became interconnected. The main contributions were: from the Bolsheviks, political discipline and the organizing of the armed forces of the revolution; from the working class, the Soviet form of organizing the civil power; the agricultural programme from the peasant party, the Socialist Revolutionaries; and the handling of industry from a consulting engineer, Grinevetsky, whose book *Post-War Perspectives of Russian Industry* had been published in 1916. This survey of the state of industry had led Grinevetsky to proposals which were fully in line with the Russian tradition of the state as the chief industrialist, and which were later developed into the planning policy of the revolutionary government. The new government also intended to continue the tradition of encouraging foreign investment in Russia, and native industrial capital was not nationalized until July 1918, when this was hurriedly done in view of the coming civil war. Management was modified by the encouragement and spread of "workers' control", which had been started by informally elected "factory committees" in factories abandoned by their owners in the February revolution. The Bolsheviks wanted to develop this into a means by which the workers could keep an eye on the management and learn the business at the same time, but this "control" worked extremely unevenly, to say the least, and did not last long. The "factory committees" were not always friendly to the trade unions, which had originated earlier and were developing rapidly after being fully legalized, for the first time, by the February government.

The first representative trade union congress was held in January 1918, and there arose a great debate on the form the movement should take. There was strong support for the policy of making the movement politically neutral and independent, that is, to transplant foreign trade unionism into Russia: the weakness in this plan was that foreign trade unionism had been moulded by the circumstances of its birth after industrial but before political revolutions, whereas the Russian trade

B

union movement was being born after a political but before an industrial revolution. The foreign trade unionism, with industrialization behind it, could take that process and the existence of a large industry for granted and could concentrate on all the questions which arise within that given framework; the newborn Russian trade unions were looking towards an intended industrialization, with all the large social questions that involved. The debate between the narrow economic and the wide social policies was settled, as in the circumstances it had to be, in favour of the social policy. This conclusion of itself raised other questions, about its actual application in trade union organization. Three policies were put forward. One extreme group wanted an industrial army, to be under a kind of military discipline with trade union organizers acting as the officers (this in effect was a highly romanticized version of an extreme direction of labour which had in part been followed during the Civil War). The other extreme wanted the trade unions to be given control of industry. This syndicalist policy was by no means as impracticable as the other, but its weakness was that it had not taken the measure of the coming industrialization. The centre policy held that, just as war is too important to be left to the soldiers, so industry is too important to be left to the trade unions: their natural and proper functions are partial and sectional, and in order to fulfil these functions their strength must not be expended in attempting those tasks which are the inevitable responsibility of society as a whole and of the state as society's executive. The Russian working class was still mostly composed of people who were not only of peasant origin but whose family ties with the villages were at the moment keeping them alive: they were in themselves both parts of society and understood the relation of the parts to the whole of their society much better than most foreign observers. It was because of this experience and understanding, and in the light of the foreknowledge that industrialization had still to come, that the two extremist policies were rejected and the centre policy adopted.

Before the first of these debates was over and while the second was still in full swing the industrial working class itself had almost disappeared, going back to the villages for food or into the new armies, as industry was ceasing on all sides of the fighting lines for lack of supplies. The country was at that time fighting for existence, in the civil war in Russia proper and in the wars of intervention in the "border" areas. These wars were among the most fantastic military activities in history: the supposed political dividing lines ran through rather than between the armies, both native and foreign. For instance, British troops in Northern Russia got in smuggled copies of *Pravda*, and insisted on the staff appointing an official interpreter to read the paper to them. In the native Russian armies even more, the political divisions ran through people's minds: and in the end it was the small group of revolutionary leaders with undivided minds who got their way, so that the class war in Russia proper ended with their victory, and the "border" wars ended with the re-establishment of approximately the Tsarist frontiers.

The cost of this fighting and its results in famine and disease were immeasurable. Industry practically disappeared; and its products became so precious that there was, for instance, a Nail Rationing Board. Naturally in these circumstances money also disappeared: goods moved through barter, through wages in kind and through armed procurements of food from the peasants to feed the armies and the towns. The element of impracticality amongst the leaders of the revolution and their politically minded followers was such that they could regard the disappearance of money transactions as the advent of communism: thus the period is still called "the period of war communism"; its other and more realistic name is "the heroic age", the age of fabulous endurance, misery, courage, ruthlessness and muddle-headedness, an age which men could hardly believe they had survived.

This amazement and high thinking reached well into the government itself, so that when the fighting was dying down, the more sober element had to struggle against the more excitable to try and normalize economic life: the armed procurements for instance were being continued in the name of communism. A sense of reality was in the end forced upon the more romantic people in the government by the mutiny in the naval base at Kronstadt, which made it plain that the change had to come immediately. The consequent re-legalization of money trade was the famous "New Economic Policy" of March 1921, announced in the form of a government statement that taxation in kind would replace the requisitioning from the peasantry. "This meant," said one Russian economist, "that the motive for sowing was restored": in other words peasants who had land and seed now became willing to grow food since they would not be robbed of it by armed squads from the towns. This new economic policy, however, did not avert one of the worst famines in Russian history, which was due not only to the weather and poor sowing but also to the lack of transport and the administrative chaos.

Industry took five years to get back to the pre-war level of production. The poverty of material resources was incredible: it is to be realized not so much in the figures and statistics, as in the things people remember doing at that time—for instance, an early agricultural commune in a dry area of the Ukraine needed an engine to pump water. So in the winter of 1926–27 three men went a hundred miles south to Perekop and scrambled about among the war debris there, found a tank and got it to move, brought it north over the melting ice, took out the engine and got the pump working. Such minor adventures were innumerable and inspired by a determination to put Russia on her feet, as is shown by the end of the same story: the water was pumped into a storage tank, and the old man who was set to watch the level of the water had to keep climbing a ladder to do so. A foreigner there made a wooden float with a circular upright painted to look like a rising sun as it came over the edge of the tank: the first time this happened, a small boy who saw it rushed off to his father to tell him about the new "American technique". There was a passion for modernization which sustained people through a heart-breaking scarcity of resources.

As the various works came back into commission, in the nationalized heavy basic industries, they were put on a profit and loss basis in the market conditions provided by the New Economic Policy. Costs of production were naturally high, and the prices of industrial products kept rising in comparison with agricultural prices, leading to the famous "scissors crisis" of

1923. Once more the "motive for sowing" was in danger of disappearing: and the crisis was only surmounted by a concentration of effort throughout nationalized industry and transport to reduce overheads and other costs of production, but the eight-hour day, which was one of the gains of the revolution, was not abandoned.

With the general completion of rehabilitation, the problems of the coming industrialization began to loom very large. The "scissors crisis" had shown that the overall social problems involved would be three: the control of agricultural production, the control of industry, and the control of relations between them. On the physical side, such control means having target figures and working to them: so after the "scissors crisis" the State Planning Commission began to develop the work of calculating annual target figures for industry as a whole, thus advancing from the planning of separate projects which had been its earlier work. These experiments in economic administration were primitive enough, and were not used by the government in its running of the country and the economy; but they did a great deal to bring home to policy-makers just what would in practice be the questions involved in the intended industrialization. There was consequently another round of furious political debates.

The question in the first stage of this round was whether Russia could industrialize on her own resources. No earlier country had done so, and all had been relatively richer in developed resources than Russia was. So two policies were put forward: one proposing to proceed to industrialization on the country's own resources, the other proposing a waiting upon or instigation of revolutions in industrial countries first so that Russian industrialization could be a more or less comfortable, parasitic and dependent process. It was naturally the first alternative that was adopted, and it was given the name of "socialism in one country".

As soon as this point was settled, the second stage of debates started, on the question from where were the necessary concentrations of wealth to be gathered? Three policies were proposed: (1) the wealth was to be gathered from the peasants and "superindustrialization" was to be rushed through; (2) industrialization was to be planned very slowly in two-year periods; and (3) industrialization was to be planned strategically in five-year periods and at the same time the collectivization of agriculture was to be steadily put through, at appropriate stages in the industrializing process when streams of labour were needed in industry, and industry could produce machines for large-scale agriculture. The superindustrialization policy received least support—in one factory meeting for example there was to have been a debate between a supporter and an opponent of superindustrialization; but when the supporter had finished his speech the floor took over the meeting and pointed out that this policy would pauperize the peasants, remove the "motive for sowing" and therefore lead to starvation in the towns and complete breakdown of the whole industrializing attempt. The floor was still speaking when the meeting closed: the platform opponent of superindustrialization never got a chance to open his mouth.

The real decision had therefore to be made between slow industrialization under partial control, and strategically planned industrialization. In April 1927 the government instructed the State Planning Commission to draw up a five-year strategic plan; and one such plan was adopted in April 1928, to take effect as from October. The intervening period was occupied by all kinds of preparations, including the printing and issuing of ration cards for use in the difficult times that were coming. The decision between slow and strategic industrialization remained in dispute: if the strategic policy failed in practice, the slow policy might take its place.

The five-year plan ratified in April 1929, six months after the work had started (so far as it could in the winter), was in broad outline a plan to develop the existing traditional industrial areas to make them capable of carrying the rest of the industrializing process. The meaning of "development" in this case was truly understood in the popular saying that it was like sewing a coat on to a button. The principal changes can be most easily realized by comparing the industrial map of 1913 (which was much the same in 1928) with that of 1932.

In 1913, Russian industry consisted of engineering and some textiles at Leningrad; machinery and large-scale textiles at and near Moscow; coal, iron and steel and railway engineering in the Donbas; ferrous and non-ferrous metals in the Urals; oil at Baku in the Caucasus; and the railway system linking these centres. The five-year plan period covered a general strengthening of this railway system and its extension to link Turkestan with Siberia; a temporary quadrupling of the industrial building labour force, and a big investment in power stations, of which Dneprostroi is the most famous among the hydro-electric developments. In the industrial centres, machine tools, turbines, textile machinery and aluminium production were intensively developed at Leningrad (running by this time on Donbas coal instead of on English as in 1913); lorries, machine tools and chemicals at Moscow; the old Donbas industries were intensively developed; tractor works were built at Kharkov, Stalingrad and Chelyabinsk, the agricultural machinery works at Rostov-on-Don was greatly expanded, and chemicals and precision engineering were begun around Dneprostroi and greatly increased elsewhere; in the Urals, the Magnitogorsk iron ore was intensively exploited; and there was a veritable oil rush at Baku. These developments in the main were the coat that was sewn on to the button. The new areas were few, the chief being Kuznets coal in Siberia, engineering in the Urals; chemicals, artificial rubber, and lorries at Gorky (Nizhni Novgorod), and a ring of industrial centres round Dneprostroi. In addition, there was some investment in consumer goods production—bakeries, footwear and ready-made clothing; but most consumer goods remained at more or less handicraft level. House-building almost ceased during the years 1929–34.

The immediate economic effects of industrialization were much less than the social: much, perhaps most, of the capital laid down did not really begin to produce until the second five-year plan period—there was, for instance, little more steel in 1932 than there was in 1913. The actual industrialization, as contrasted with the official Plan and the planning policies of previous years, consisted in complete concentration on intensive development of key projects at the cost of consumer goods industries and housing, so the intensive development actually got further than had been foreseen, and "the plan" was "completed in four years" (in fact the old talk of "super-industrialization" was made to look small by what actually occurred). On the other hand, consumer goods other than the barest essentials disappeared, which had not been intended. The comparative stability of average output per head is remarkable, in view of the flood of unskilled and dilutee labour which came into industry at this time, and the collapse in the standard of living.

The unskilled labour consisted in part of peasants who customarily came to town in the agricultural off-season; some of it consisted of peasants who had never seen a town before, and unskilled is a mild term—as witness the country lad who was told to paint the outside of the windows and did so, glass and all. Dilutee labour in the skilled trades was in part put through crude training courses; but the previous level of productivity was in fact kept up by the efforts of the existing industrial workers: in a Kharkov factory for example, skilled men commonly worked for two and three shifts on end, and the record was held by an engineer who did not leave the works for three weeks while a machine was being assembled. The barbarity of the wastage inevitable in these circumstances cannot be overestimated; precious imported machinery was often wrecked in a few days. This was not only due to unskilled labour; the Russian industrial technicians had a tradition of their own which is best summed up in John Littlepage's story of the mining engineers who expected to do their day's work without soiling their white gloves. Such men were prepared to worship but not to work the fine imported machines and had unlimited contempt for the workers who ruined them; but they would have been, in a gentlemanly way, revolted by the coarseness of Lancashire's industrializing proverb: "where there's muck, there's brass". The Russian industrialization consequently had to produce not only a skilled working class but also a new technical class: and some of the latter were exceedingly rough diamonds, and proud of it. These social processes were well begun in the first five-year plan, so that the social products came out of the new factories and mines more quickly than did the material products.

The very high labour turnover and mobility of the period

was partly necessary (in the construction gangs) and partly an aspect of the general excitement and restlessness. The physical separation of men from their families, and the change from a rural to an industrial way of life, bring inescapable problems: in our industrialization two main problems are typified by the way of life in Gin Lane, and the use of the London mob by Wilkes; in America, the corresponding folklore types are the wild west and Tammany Hall. In the Russian industrialization the phenomena in these social fields were the factory clubs, which extended from the sordid to the more than magnificent and took the place of the gin palaces and saloons elsewhere; the Trade Unions, which handled the work of the friendly societies and the social side of Tammany; and the Communist Party which took the place of mob organization or Tammany politics, and was itself transformed in the process, as we shall see later. Nor was the grim God-fearingness of other industrializations lacking, though it appeared in Russia in a different way: it is the emotional basis of Stalinist orthodoxy on the one hand, and of the cleaning up of the family and abortion laws on the other, and of many similar processes in the thirties.

The wealth invested during the first five-year plan was collected and concentrated partly by state savings from agricultural and industrial production from 1926, and partly by reduction of the standard of living during the years 1928 onwards. This was the time when people went more than short, for agricultural products were exported to buy essential machinery from abroad just when, during the world depression, international agricultural prices fell much more than industrial prices. The situation in the Odessa shipyards is summed up in the memory of hungry men watching the grain ships put to sea and bidding farewell to their bread, while two days of diligent telephonic search were required to obtain a pound of flour to make paste for paper-hanging. The flow of physical products from the new mines and factories was not established till 1934; but two years later the new industry was self-providing and machinery imports almost ceased by 1937. This means that in the years 1934–36 industry itself was producing a stream of capital goods, and the old problem of saving up for investment by the state over several years was in principle ended. This had three main results: first, investment was now directed to machinery (especially new types for mechanizing other industries and agriculture), to coal and power stations, to technical improvement as well as enlargement in the steel industry, to non-ferrous metals and chemicals, and—in consumer goods—to food processing and footwear, together with a slow resumption of housing. Also at this time there was made the first beginning of modern industry in the non-Slav parts of the U.S.S.R., as in the big cotton mill at Tashkent in Uzbekistan, and the locomotive works at Ulan Ude in Buryat Mongolia (Eastern Siberia).

The second result was the birth of a newly skilled working class, armed with the stream of equipment beginning to flow from basic industry. A newly skilled working class is a very different phenomenon from a working class old in traditional experience: the Russian workers had a fierce pride in their new hands, and a deep and innocent reverence for the three whole generations of skill that lay behind a Leningrad worker. I came home one day in Moscow to find my room-mate had a visitor, a middle-aged man carrying his authority for all to see; he was introduced with honour as a Leningrad worker, and promptly brought out a gold watch presented to him by the Leningrad party and Soviet for excellent work. It was only then that I learned he was a factory director, in our terms an important industrialist: this counted for less in his mind and my room-mate's than that he was a Leningrad worker, to whom the pride of having a skilled industrial trade was a family tradition going back as far as his grandfather. It was out of such a newly skilled working class that the "Stakhanovite movement" came as the first realization that the new hands not only had skills, but that these skills could be organized with economy and precision. This sudden discovery of beauty in the muck and sweat of a harsh and unkindly process was not something that could be talked about directly without embarrassment, but it is the hidden spring of a great deal of the vulgar nonsense written in Russia about the dignity and heroism of labour, and no less of the dour primness that often measures personal worth in terms of the political and other orthodoxies that keep this secret beauty safe. Only once, to my knowledge, has it approached direct expression, and that in a tale of craftsmen of the olden days, the film *The Stone Flower*. It will come out, as these things do, when it has had time to become comfortable and familiar; too few people in Russia as yet know about it and live with it for the shyness about it to disappear.

The third result of the new flow of production in 1934–36 was that rationing could be ended and consumption standards in food restored. And also there was an article of communal conspicuous consumption, the famous Moscow underground, which is probably the real and inarticulate manifesto that the joy of industrial skill and the beauty of its use are known.

The dour and roaring years of 1929–36 changed the face and the heart of Russia. They had been long in preparation, and the people of the towns went down into their material and physical misery unreluctantly on the whole; they found there a greater cost than they had foreseen, but they also found a new kind of human worth: and Russian life and Soviet politics have been trying to come to terms with this new thing ever since.

The rest of the story of industrialization is for the most part well known, especially how the industry was tested by the war and spread eastwards to new areas. The utter weariness and discouragement with which people faced the sight of everything to be rebuilt is not so widely appreciated, so that it is often not seen how this mood changed to amazement, energy and cocksureness when experience showed that rebuilding is a very different and very much easier thing than industrialization. This relief and new-found confidence set the tone for post-war industry, which is now very much richer, more varied and widespread and technically far superior to what it was in 1941.

CHAPTER III

FARMING AND ITS CHANGES

FOR centuries the wealth of Russia has lain in her agricultural produce. She has been in this period a poor country because the good rainfall comes on poor soils, while the good soils have an unreliable rainfall: so Russia is traditionally a famine country, and the workers on the land have been both materially and politically weak. This gave a particular form to her feudalism, capitalism and early socialism, and accounts for many historical peculiarities, as compared with the development of central and western Europe. For example, when the salt monopolist Stroganov sent an annexing Cossack force into Siberia in the sixteenth century, he wanted not wool or wheat, but furs, in other words to extend a luxury trade at home on the basis of hunting, not farming, in the new area. This organizational combination of luxury and lack of production is familiar in Russian history.

But the basic central areas have of course been the productive areas on which the development of Russia has been grounded; and up until the recent industrialization their products have been in the main agricultural. Agricultural wealth in any state consists of two principal sectors: the products which are eaten or worn on the farm, and the products which go off the farm in the form of dues and taxes under feudalism, in the form of rent and taxes and sales under capitalism, and in the form of taxes, payment in kind and sales under Early Soviet Socialism. The proportion of on-farm to off-farm within the total product depends on the technology and organization of agriculture, and on the organization of the economic and political system as a whole.

The predominant technology of Russian farming until the end of the nineteenth century was the ordinary mediaeval kind: the village possessed the land, which it distributed in strips among its members. The villagers ploughed the strips with the *sokha*, the wooden plough that was so much a member of the family that it had a name "Andrew", which was also that of Russia's apostle. The strips were not hedged or fenced, and there was an elementary fallow rotation; so the village as a community (the *mir*) fixed times of ploughing, sowing, harvesting and pasturing. This village self-government was as independent of state government in old feudal Russia as in feudal Britain; and in the same way the two governments were bound together by custom and law which regulated the passing of off-farm produce to the feudal lords, the church, and the state.

Feudal organization as we understand the term broke down in Russia during the seventeenth century in a welter of civil wars, changes of dynasty, peasant revolts, and schisms in the church. The underlying problem was to find a way of increasing the size of the off-farm product in order to have more goods for the developing trade, and this was done not by improving farming technique or organization (as in the main happened in this country), but by increasing off-farm exactions at the cost of on-farm consumption. At first this took the form of increasing feudal exaction: serfdom became more and more inescapable until in 1649 a runaway serf was pursued till the end of his life and could find no lawful refuge anywhere. But even this was not enough, and serfdom became chattel slavery when in 1675 there was the first of a series of enactments which legalized the selling of serfs off the land and without their families. This chattel slavery system continued in force fully till 1801 and in part till 1861.

Thus the period 1675–1861 is in Russia a period of postfeudal chattel slavery which increases the amount of off-farm produce and by this means develops the market organization of internal and foreign trade in agricultural and early industrial goods. This form of transition from feudalism to capitalism is not unique: there was the same use of chattel slavery in the southern states of the U.S.A. and our own Barbadoes. In Russia this slavery meant (as it meant elsewhere) that the relations between owner and owned and between on-farm and off-farm wealth were not regulated by custom or law, that exactions were arbitrary. In addition, from the early eighteenth

century onwards the owners were also the tax-gatherers for the
state.

Even while this system was being introduced the Russians
were deeply ashamed of it—even those Russians who were
doing the introducing. Peter the Great in 1721 said: "The
owners sell their peasants and domestics not even in families
but one by one, like cattle, as is done nowhere else in the whole
world, from which practice there is not a little wailing" and
instructed that "this type of sale should cease, or if that is
impossible" at least people should be sold in whole families.
In 1767 Catherine deprived the slaves of their last legal rights by
enacting that anyone petitioning against his master should be
knouted and sent to the mines for life. When Catherine wrote of
the civilizing of Russia under her rule, she did not mention this
law; and, throughout the period and after, Russian educated
people in general either passed over or whitewashed the whole
system, as Mackenzie Wallace found when he was in Russia
shortly after Emancipation (vol. II, 1905 edition, pp. 236–7).
This tradition of shamed silence continues even among educated
Soviet Russians: Lyashchenko for instance, in his very detailed
economic history, does not mention the chattelization laws,
the market in human commodities, or the use of this market
as a threat to hold down the slaves, to decrease on-farm
consumption and increase the off-farm product. Consequently
the furious academic debates on when capitalism came to
Russia concentrate on the development of industry (which
was very small) and the laws leading to the internal free market
in 1762; and these discussions are inevitably unreal. Of course,
it is praiseworthy that the Russians should be as ashamed of the
enslavement of their countrymen as we are ashamed of the
sending of English and Irish peasants to slavery in the West
Indies and of the "Killing Times" in Scotland: but in both
Britain and Russia the facts of how capitalism came should not
be missed out of the history books.

The development of enslavement continued in Russia
until about half the agricultural labour force was reduced
to slavery: the rest remained serfs on Crown lands with considerably more regular lives, a greater personal freedom, and
less arbitrary interference in the exercise of local self-govern-

ment in the village *mirs*. After Tsar Paul (1796–1801) separated
the Privy Purse lands from the Crown lands, there began a
revulsion against further enslavement: grants transferring
Crown lands to private owners (and so changing the serfs
into slaves) gradually came to an end. In 1801, the selling of
slaves off the land became illegal, though the sale of domestic
slaves continued freely. The treatment of slaves by their
masters began to come under legal cognisance; there were
local and limited emancipations; and general emancipation
began to be mooted. Serf self-government on the Crown lands
was slightly enlarged by the organization of *mirs* into *volosts*
joining several *mirs* together for juridical purposes, so that the
volost courts administered the old unwritten peasant law. But
there seems to have been no development of a practical palatine
administration on the Crown lands, that is, a progressive
technology or organization of farming by diversification or
specialization (as happened in the English Crown lands during
the fourteenth and fifteenth centuries).

On the slave lands, compulsory labour service varied from
three days a week (legalised in 1797) to seven days a week on
some estates. This system provided the capital that was
invested in industry during the eighteenth century, and also
allowed for a considerable growth of population: the area
that in Peter's time carried 13,000,000 people carried more than
twice that number by the end of Catherine's reign seventy-four
years later. It is likely therefore that the total amount of on-farm
consumption increased while its proportion of the whole
product may have fallen (there are no statistics for the period):
but this is uncertain because so much of off-farm consumption
was by domestic slaves and other forms of non-agricultural
labour-power in the retinues of the nobles. The increase in the
total agricultural product presumably came almost entirely
from bringing newly cleared forest and woodland under the
plough.

Far too much of the off-farm product in this period was
wasted by vicious and absentee owners, and this enters into
the economy only negatively, as a delay in capital accumulation.
A larger amount still was expended in the first place in conspicuous consumption by the nobles, but this wealth in some

part passed into the Russian market in one way or another, and helped to develop market organization: the other part was fixed in the building of rural palaces and the like, and so passed out of production. This conspicuous consumption was organizationally wasteful, for concentrations of wealth were dispersed by such expenditure, and had to be gathered together again before they could be applied to investment. For these two reasons, although the market developed, investment proceeded slowly, and the chattel slave system was corroded by the suppressed but struggling market rather than supplanted by a reorganization of wealth. The way in which market organization forces its way into production in the early part of the nineteenth century is seen in several economic phenomena: there is to a very limited extent the orthodox capitalist method of working an estate with wage-labour: this is rare. Another method was to employ the slaves full-time in labour service and give subsistence wages in kind: this high-water mark of slavery was also rare. More frequently there was a mixed system, by which individuals or *mirs* commuted labour-service for money rent: they acquired the money by wage-labour in industry or agriculture, by industrial outwork in consumer goods production, or by the marketing of peasant produce. Merchant capital also began to appear in agriculture in the worst possible form: merchants would buy estates, strip them of timber and all fixed capital, and leave them ruined. Similarly, in the south and the steppes merchant capital would cultivate and crop land for three or four years then leave it exhausted to lie fallow for a generation. To these irregularities of production was added a necessary irregularity of trade: the owner of an estate desired to change his off-farm product into money, but he had no money measure of the costs of production, so that the price he accepted was often very wide of any economic valuation because he could employ uncosted slave labour for transport to distant markets as well as for production. Thus in the later years of the chattel slavery period, the activities of the owners were always tending to destroy the market organization, and merchant capital in agriculture tended to destroy agriculture. It was this conflict within the system itself which caused the inefficiences revealed by the Crimean War, and led to the freeing of the Crown serfs and abolition of slavery in a series of measure from 1859 to 1866, of which the chief, abolishing slavery, was the law of 19th February, 1861.

It was only gradually after Emancipation that market organization fully triumphed over other forces, which were represented within Emancipation itself. For example, the compensation to their former owners imposed on the peasants was often wide of the economic mark, so that in some areas peasants were kept on the land by the *mirs* against the individual's will or interests, and in other areas were driven off against their own interests or those of the developing economy as a whole. Secondly, the form in which the compensation was paid out to the farm owners (government bonds redeemable after fifteen years) discouraged the very necessary capital investment on the now smaller estates, though in the longer run the owners reaped the benefit of good land, compact and balanced farm economies and the rise in land values, so that their off-farm product remained high and often increased. Thirdly, the freed peasants constituted a productive labour-force of great energy (the average yield rose steeply during the second half of the nineteenth century), but this national asset appreciated in value by the sweat of peasants working for themselves, without much benefit of capital investment. Thus the huge wheat exports of the 1890s which paid for machinery and other imports were due to the estate economies, to concentration on grain crops, but mostly to the freed peasants' sweat. It was also this newly released savage human energy that produced from the unskilled construction gangs in railway building the new type of capitalist in Russia, who is no more than a blown-up gang boss; it was this element, together with representatives of the older merchant capital (Dostoievsky's trader-notables) and a few of the nobles, which constituted the capitalist class of Russia from 1861 to 1917. The most notorious representative of this ex-peasant type in high places is Rasputin.

In the upshot, the non-economic features of Emancipation served to feed and enlarge the economic differentiation in the countryside which follows naturally from capitalist organization. This differentiation was consequently very rapid in

c

Russia: the *average* rural standard of living materially, and more especially in security, was probably worsened by Emancipation. (There is a Russian proverb: "The slave drinks beer, the free man water.") This process of differentiation was hastened by Stolypin's measures in 1906–10, which freed the go-ahead peasant from the *mir*, fostered a kulak class, and fully exposed the villages to the strong cold winds of the market.

Thus over the generations from 1861 to 1917, the mass of the peasantry had good current reasons for dissatisfaction, but all these were merely additions to their main grievance, which was their stubborn conviction that the compensation payable on Emancipation merely continued the previous lawless situation existing since the seventeenth century. It is impossible to overestimate the importance of this popular historical and legal doctrine in the peasants' minds: for them, it contained and explained every current difficulty and disaster, until in 1917 they left the army in their millions, went home, and took the landowners' land. This action was legalized by the revolutionary government on 8th November, 1917, the day after it took power. The revolutionary government thus became the first law-abiding government for nearly three centuries.

This happy legality and peasant self-assertion raised the most serious problems in the relations between on-farm consumption and the off-farm product, and these were exacerbated by the civil wars and wars of intervention. As already mentioned, during the years 1918–21, the armies and towns lived off the countryside by organizing armed squads which procured grain by force on information received from Committees of the Village Poor (deserving and undeserving) that were organized by the local government authorities. Three centuries of skill in avoiding and evading exactions stood the peasants in good stead at this time; but this skill was in part circumvented by the organizational device of setting the village poor against the rest. The result of the total situation was one of the worst famines in Russia history in 1921–22. It is a remarkable tribute to all concerned that agricultural production was about restored in the four years 1923–26, and that the off-farm sector was capable of feeding the reconstituted industrial labour-force.

During this period, the organization of agriculture had

been transformed. The peasant appropriations of 1917 had broken up most of the estates, and thus brought a considerable part of the previous off-farm sector into the on-farm sector. The armed procurements reversed this process by forcing grain off the farms, and yet broke up the large peasant households which were the chief off-farm producers after 1917: a peasant household of ten members owning four horses was much more likely to keep its beasts if it split into two households each with two horses. These processes, added to war and famine, meant that by 1921 the off-farm sector of agriculture had almost disappeared. The taxation which replaced the armed procurements was therefore heavy, but this did not, apparently, affect the peasant's view that the land was theirs at last, and that taxation was much more law-abiding than armed procurements. It was on this basis that production got under way again, and that differentiation within the peasantry recommenced: by 1925 there were farms of a size needing hired labour to work them, and such employment was made legal again.

When a working class comes to power in the towns, it is faced with the decision whether it is going to socialize agriculture, or whether agriculture is going to bring capitalism back. The politicians of the Russian working class had no doubts what the decision ought to be; and in addition they firmly believed that only if Russian agricultural production was organized in large units could there be made the capital investment required to raise productivity and end the traditional status of Russia as a famine country. Consequently, during the peasant appropriations of 1917–18 the government tried to keep estates undivided and operate them as state farms; and a statement on collectivization policy (of which no one took the slightest notice) was incorporated in the Land Law of February 1918. By 1922 agricultural production was organized in family holdings almost exclusively, and the immediate problem of encouraging the growth of the off-farm sector, however organized, was paramount. By 1927 however taxation and the market were bringing the off-farm sector forward, and the question of socializing agriculture became practical for the first time.

The first problem was to introduce to the peasantry at

large the conception of the agricultural product as a social product in something at least of the sense in which an industrial (as distinct from a handicraft) product is a social product. This involved two aspects: the technical means (machinery); and the organization of the producers. Russia was poor in machinery, so the most was made of what was available: a state farm was provided with tractor power, which it both used for itself and hired out to its neighbour peasants; this was used as a showplace for peasant delegations; machine-hiring groups of poor (horseless) peasants were formed in selected areas, and tractors loaned to them. On the organizational side, several forms of combined working were encouraged: (1) the commune, in which all property was communal; (2) the artel or collective, in which land, labour, horses and machinery were pooled; and (3) the co-operative, in which for certain limited purposes work and funds were pooled. At the same time, legal and fiscal discrimination against the better-off peasants employing wage-labour was increased. The effect of this latter policy was a slow but steady reduction in off-farm grain during the years 1926–29, at the same time as the industrial labour-force was growing.

It was after the 1929 harvest was in that the government decided to press forward collectivization in the main grain areas through the winter of 1929–30 in time for the spring ploughing. The development was planned as a political campaign for "the dissolution of the kulakry" and was intended as a replacement of the kulaks by collective farms as the main producers of off-farm grain. The secondary grain areas were to be collectivized by the spring of 1932, and the most difficult areas by the autumn of 1933. This was the plan for a "revolution from above" adopted on 5th January, 1930.

The political machine swung into action, and it very quickly became plain that the machine was running away with the plan. The machine in this case consisted in the main of young industrial workers fired by a mixture of political enthusiasm and the industrializing fever of the towns, generally with a woeful ignorance of agricultural processes, but a very certain knowledge of their own and their families' current privations, and the townsman's tendency to regard the countryman as slow and stupid. They found in some areas kindred spirits in the "young communist" lads in the villages: the fate of one village was settled by such lads coming over from a neighbouring village one night and stripping the houses of all moveable goods, which they auctioned in their own village the next day. In another case, the personal confidence of the local politician terrified a village into believing, on his word alone, that if they did not collectivize immediately he would designate them all as kulaks and order their transportation to Siberia. In other cases, tension in the village between the kulaks and the rest was so great that kulak families were torn apart and their children left to fend for themselves and die by themselves. In brief, there was a serious miscalculation by these townsmen of the degree to which the countryside shared the passion for modernization, and consequently the drive they themselves had to show to put collectivization through; as a result the movement went much too far both in communalizing all property, and in the number of peasants collectivized, and signs of peasant revolt appeared. In March and April the government had to allow peasants to leave the farms, and if they remained in, to resume ownership of their own kitchen gardens and livestock where these had been communalized. But a great deal of harm had been done both materially (in the slaughtering of beasts) and politically in the loss of peasant confidence in the government, to say nothing of the human disasters in the transportation of kulak families, while the famines or near-famines of 1930–32 were organizational and not climatic in origin. The reaction of a considerable body of the peasantry is summed up in the story of the old countrywoman who visited the tomb of Lenin (the leader of the first law-abiding government for three centuries) to pray his intercession for his people against the wicked Bolsheviks.

A great deal has been said and written about the ugly side of collectivization, and it should be the job of history books to try and decide whether, overall, it was a good or bad thing, and whether it was carried through well or badly. In answering the first question the main consideration to be borne in mind is that large historical movements are in the end always judged by their long-term effects—whether they

provide, or lay the foundations for providing, a better life
for the people who survive them. The first question can
now be answered without much doubt: collectivization soon
provided a better life for the townspeople; it also by 1936
was able to prevent the coming into existence of famine in the
countryside; and it certainly laid the foundations for the long-
needed capitalization of Russian agriculture. A small part of
this capital investment was made straight away, in the establishment and building up of the network of machine and tractor
stations: this capitalized grain growing, and so made a basis for
further mechanization. The thorough capitalization of agriculture, however, necessarily had to wait until industry could
provide the machines and fertilizers; that is, until after the war
and rehabilitation; it also had to wait until collective work
could be organized on a fully economic basis, instead of
the mixture of a new economic and a traditional village and
family basis in the first collectivization. This establishment
of a fully economic basis was carried through in the amalgama-
tions of 1950 and succeeding years, so that for the first time in
Russian history farming could be both large-scale and diversified
(for centuries, cereals formed well over 90 per cent of the crop
area). The greatness of the need for capitalization in Russian
agriculture can be measured by one figure alone: the cereal
yield is on the average a third of ours; and while the yield in
Russia and U.S.A. is about the same, it takes something like
six times the number of people to get it out of the soil in Russia.
So the history book's answer to the first question should be:
there have been some good results from collectivization so far;
and with the present heavy capital investment in agriculture
there ought to be a vast improvement in productivity, yield,
diversification and specialization, and standard of life both
in the towns and the countryside. That is the narrow but long-
term and therefore not yet certain answer to the question; the
broader but certain answer is that collectivization or something
very like it was essential to the new industrial system and its
speed of growth, without which Russia would be an appendage,
not a conqueror, of Nazism.

The second question is whether collectivization was
carried through well or badly. We have already seen that it

was not carried through on the government's plan; and since most of the human and material destruction was due to haste, the government cannot be blamed for this so far as its plan goes. And certainly there is no "hidden hand" or Providence to take the blame. The process was however planned by the government as a thorough political and organizational campaign, and the campaigners were both selected and briefed by the government. So far as we know anything about the briefing, it was wholly in conformity with the general plan of campaign, which was public, and which was also the crowning point of a long series of laws and propaganda-information, not to mention ferocious party disputes which had very thoroughly ventilated the question and various policies about it. But the selection of the campaigners as young men who had recently grown up in the new town-life, and who would be temperamentally less sympathetic to the old country ways than older men, must have been deliberate on the government's part; so that both the selectors and those selected must bear the blame for the worse aspects of collectivization, just as they share the praise for its better ones. But of course the countryfolk were not merely passive in the process: some qualities of theirs also must have contributed to the way it went, to its basic completion in ten weeks instead of the planned three years.

This difference between plan and performance alone is evidence that the mass of the country people were readier than was thought to embark on a new, modern, way of life; and in addition there is no doubt that the meaning of kulak had changed since the beginning of the century, and that in some areas at least it changed during collectivization. I once asked a dozen or so ex-campaigners and others from various parts of the country what a kulak was; and they gave the answers each for their own region, and were surprised at each other's replies: they had not before realized that the variations in the different parts of the country were so great. These variations referred mainly to areas of land owned, and also to numbers of horses and of hired labourers, and other statistical quantities. But there was something else which was common to the definitions, and much more important: this was what might be called the kulak quality of mind and the kulak attitude to fellow-villagers. I mentioned above the savage energy released by Emancipation and the kind of industrial capitalist it produced; in quality of mind and social attitude the kulak was that kind of capitalist in the village. Thus, a man owning land and horses and hiring labour, but not oppressing his fellow villagers was not, in the general estimation, a "fist"; while a grasping bully who was poorer in productive wealth but harder on his hired man and who ground the faces of the poor who borrowed horses, grain or money from him was most definitely a kulak. This mixture of statistical and social definitions was clear enough in each village; but when the young townsmen arrived, the mixed definition tended to spill over to include anyone who opposed them, for whatever motive: this was why the threat could be made to designate a whole village as "kulaks". The reason is obvious: for a young townsman, a kulak was rather vaguely conceived as a peasant who set his immediate private interests above the long-term modern common good: collectivization was the long-term modern common good, therefore its opponents were kulaks.

Given the miscalculation of readiness to modernize in the countryside, and the kind of campaigner selected in consequence, both the unexpected speed, and the wretched miseries of the process as it actually happened, were natural results. Such a combination of forces and their collisions is of course of a kind that is very difficult to understand from outside a country; from inside, where the forces are visibly real people, they may be deplored and cursed, but they look quite natural and not at all mysterious, and whatever sorrow and hate may be engendered, everyone knows that with patience and endurance things will sort themselves out. This does not, of course, mean that everyone knows which side will win in the end: and in fact after collectivization the countryfolk remained undecided for some years. The shift of opinion probably began when the famine of 1936 did not materialize (as, from the weather, it should have done); in 1937 an old peasant who was a fellow patient of mine in hospital told me that, taking all in all, he had concluded that Stalin was a truly great man, like Lenin. This shift of opinion had proceeded far enough by the time the war came for Russia to emerge victorious; and may be expected to move far more quickly now as the stream of investment flows into agriculture and changes both life in the countryside and the relations of that life with the towns and cities.

Up to the end of Early Soviet Socialism, the stream of wealth flowing from the farms to the towns was far greater than the stream of agricultural machinery, fertilizers and manufactured consumer goods flowing from the towns to the villages. Collectivization made possible a very large increase in off-farm grain, with nothing like a corresponding increase of farm production. This was the main immediate purpose of collectivization, but the memory of it in rural malnutrition will not long survive the fruition of the longer-term purpose of collectivization that has now begun: this is the pouring into the countryside of a stream of equipment and skill, a return, as it were, for the grain that fed the industrial workers while they were making the industry that can now so richly supply the countryside with its own long-needed investment.

If, as is likely, the peasants of Russia are willing to make good use of this industrial assistance within the collective system of farming, the greatest political effects of collectivization will be felt on the world scale within a generation from now. The brutalities and hazards of its breakneck origin in Russia will be forgotten and the peasant majority of the world's population may see in it the surest way of calling industry and science to their aid. The coming social and industrial revolutions of the world are likely to be profoundly influenced in this way amongst others by Russian experience.

CHAPTER IV

RUNNING THE FARMS AND FACTORIES

IN the first years of collectivized farming the internal organization of the new farms was experimental, and in many of them chaotic. It was in this period that the "collective farm compromise" was worked out: over nine-tenths of the arable area in each farm is worked collectively with machines from the local Machine and Tractor Station and with horses owned by the farm; the remaining area is divided into "household plots" at the cottage door, of about an acre or less for each family. By 1935 a system on these lines had crystallized sufficiently for the government to issue a detailed set of "Model Rules" which are still the legal basis of collective farming, and provide the standard pattern for the internal organization of the farms.

Each farm holds a written title (with map) for the land it occupies. These are most imposing and magnificent documents; they state that the land is at the disposal of the farm in perpetuity and rent free. This legal formula was designed so that it would remain unchanged through changes either in the form or in the proportion of the off-farm product. Since 1935 the off-farm product has comprised (1) payment in kind to the state for the work of the Machine and Tractor Stations (MTS) which are owned by the state and each of which serves several farms; (2) "compulsory deliveries" of some kinds of farm produce, in proportions and at prices fixed by the central authorities for each main agricultural zone of the country, and fixed in detail for each farm by the local authorities; (3) contracts made before the harvest by the state and co-operative purchasing departments with each farm for deliveries after the harvest; (4) free sales at whatever prices the townspeople are willing to pay in collective farm markets or bazaars in the towns.

In these categories of the off-farm product, the payment in kind for MTS work was originally intended as a fair payment for the work done, but soon became the main device for getting grain off the farms. The "compulsory deliveries" are paid for at so low a price that they are really a tax in kind; they apply to food crops such as grain and meat, not to industrial crops such as cotton, flax and sugar beet, which the state has encouraged by paying relatively good prices for them under the contract system. The payment in kind and the compulsory deliveries have legal priority over all other off-farm movements and on-farm consumption, so that many grain farms have done no more than fulfil their quotas, and have had nothing left to distribute among their members. The poorest farms have limped along on seed and fodder borrowed from their neighbours or from the state. Average farms produce enough to sell on contract and at the markets, while the rich farms have big contract or market sales: average and rich farms therefore can (after setting aside fodder, seed and a legally fixed minimum proportion of income for reserves and investment) make distribution to their members in kind and cash which vary from the small to the sizeable.

Legally, each farm is a self-governing unit. In fact, however, the actual independence of a farm varies according to its ability to fulfil its off-farm deliveries to the state procurements centre: it has been the primary duty of the local government and communist party officials in agricultural areas to see that these deliveries are made. These officials interfere, to whatever extent is necessary and feasible, in the internal affairs of a backward farm.

We have already mentioned the young townsmen who pushed collectivization through. Their official and legal position was that they staffed the "political departments" of the newly established MTS. Their duties were to organize the new farms and get the off-farm product coming forward, and for this purpose in the beginning they were often armed, and all other local officials of any description were subordinated to them. After 1935, normal local government was resumed. The Village Soviets are the lowest rung of the local government ladder and have little power; in the ordinary way they covered three or four farms, but since the amalgamation of collective farms in 1950 most Village Soviets cover a single farm. Above them are the District Soviets with considerable legal power and with actual power as the vehicles of the District party committee. In the more densely populated parts of the country, a rural district now comprises several thousand families in about twenty farms, served by two or three MTS. Few districts had more than a few score communist party members before the war, and most of these were officials and technicians in the district town; nowadays nearly all the farms have party branches. The chief communist party official, the senior secretary of the district party committee, is usually the man who really runs the district and is still usually a townsman. Until recently his career depended above all on the extent and promptness with which his district fulfilled its off-farm obligations; but now his responsibilities to the population of the district are assuming a greater importance.

Above the district, and rather remote and awesome to the ordinary folk, is the Province Soviet, with the corresponding province party committee. At province level, agriculture and industry meet: the 130 senior secretaries of the province party committees have a strong claim to be regarded as the men who keep Russia running. The Provincial Agricultural Departments are departments of the Ministry of Agriculture, and are administrative and technical bodies; their heads are usually members of the Provincial Soviet and on the Provincial party committee. The Provincial Agricultural Department is the cornerstone of agricultural planning, in the sense that the national agricultural plans rely on its knowledge of the local situation; and in the parcelling out of the plan through each province, it advises the Provincial Soviet on the capacities of each district. The district offices of the department, in turn, advise the District Soviet on the capacities of each farm. A farm settles its plan (the basis of which is its crop acreages) when its chairman is interviewed by the executive of the District Soviet, which has the final authority to fix the plan of each farm and is advised on the technical side by the district agricultural office.

Both before the war and since, technical problems have

been subordinate to problems of personnel, morale and organization on the farms: these are the responsibility of the political people, and their views have been always and universally paramount. Consequently the rhythm of agricultural life in Russia is marked by the seasonal "campaigns" of the autumn ploughing, winter work such as snow retention and construction jobs, spring ploughing and sowing, summer harvest and state deliveries. These campaigns have been run by the district political people from outside the farms; they urge on the farms and MTS, check on work done, sack farm chairmen and get others appointed, expedite the state deliveries and lend an intrusive hand all round. After the war, the district political people were similarly in charge of the rehabilitation of agriculture; then from 1950 onwards they put through the government's decision to "amalgamate" the old collectives. This reduced the number of agricultural units by putting on the average three farms into one. The resulting size of farm is such that it is a complex production unit with very considerable potentialities for internal diversification and specialization: consequently the tendency is away from the peasant jack of all trades (and all of them somewhat simple) towards farm workers specializing in particular branches and with an increasing familiarity with machinery and science on the farm. The one very special trade of managing these large production units remains the particular interest of the political people, but the conditions of their work have been changed both for better and worse by amalgamation. For example, nearly all the new farms now have substantial party branches among their members, so that the District political people are no longer merely intrusive. Again, when a large farm is successful it is an entity of substance and weight and is not likely to take unwarranted interference meekly. On the other hand, an unsuccessful farm affects the lives of more people and is a much more serious liability to a district: it is now not so easy as it was to get rid of one of "the party boys" at the District town who happens to be under a cloud by putting him into a farm as chairman and hoping for the best. As a result of all these new conditions, rural rank and file public opinion has become a force in its own right over the past few years:

successful farms must be treated with respect, and unsuccessful ones can no longer be merely bullied.[1]

The new farms still have the same form of internal self-government as the old. The big event of the year is the annual general meeting of all members in the late winter, when all accounts have been made up and the net proceeds of the collective work are known. The district party and agricultural offices are normally represented at these meetings by senior officials; the members hear reports on the year's work from the outgoing Board of Management and Checking Commission; the new elections to these bodies take place and the year's dividend is declared.

The dividend is in the form of the value of a labour-day,

[1]During 1954, while this book was in the press, further important improvements were made in the collective farms' conditions, especially in the grain areas, where most of the farms are situated. The chief improvement is a reduction and standardization at a flat rate of payment in kind for the work done by the Machine and Tractor Stations, and a reduction in the amount of compulsory deliveries. These reductions will leave the farms with much more of their produce to do as they please with, and the state now offers to buy part of this new disposable surplus, presumably at a price high enough to make such sales worthwhile to the farms. One reason why, early in 1954, the government decided to plough up over thirty million acres of idle land is probably that, when it recognized the political necessity of making these concessions to the grain farms, it had to find a quick alternative source of off-farm grain to make up for increased on-farm consumption by the farmers and their animals.

The "new lands" are being run mostly as state farms, though credit facilities and tax exemptions are offered to encourage collective farming too. The government's intention is to develop these areas permanently and to bring eventually about seventy-five million acres into use, mostly in Southern Siberia and Kazakhstan. The whole campaign, so far, is reminiscent of the first five-year plan in its appeal for voluntary migration of young people to pioneering areas; it is different, however, in that the purpose is a quick increase in food supplies instead of heavy industry, and that large industrial resources (in tractors, pre-fabricated buildings, water piping, light railway construction and so forth) can be switched to this purpose. Official statements and press reports in the autumn of 1954 indicate much hardship and much success, but how the whole project will turn out, in comparison, say, with the British ground-nuts scheme in Africa, remains to be seen. Expert western opinion is dubious, but the Russians have a better knowledge of their own climate, soil, agricultural science and social energy. Some such decision was, however, forced on the government by the simultaneous insistence of both the townspeople and the farmers for an improvement in their standard of living quicker than the plans announced during 1952 and 1953 could provide for. Another big difference from early Soviet Socialism is that the days when difficult new areas can be pioneered with convict or exile labour are as dead as Botany Bay.

which is a unit not of time but of work according to principles laid down by the government. A day's "ordinary" work such as that of a carter or of a stableman or dairymaid with little experience counts as one labour-day, while a day's work that can be done by juveniles is half a labour-day, and the most skilled, responsible or experienced farmers can earn two labour-days or more in one day's work. The total dividend is decided by first allocating seed, fodder and reserves out of the on-farm produce, and cash for investment, insurance and reserves out of money earnings. The remainder is the net on-farm product and this is divided by the total number of labour-days earned in the year, and is shared out, in kind and cash, to each member according to the labour-days standing to his or her credit in the farm accountant's books. The value of a labour-day is the index of a farm's prosperity, and a chairman under whom this is high will normally be re-elected year after year with the blessing of the District political authorities.

The normal work teams in the farms are now "brigades" of fifty to eighty people responsible for particular fields or branches of work such as stockbreeding or building. The leadership of these brigades is the real training ground in organization within the farms. The key job of farm chairman is filled from three main sources: these farm "brigadiers", agricultural or technical experts, and the old party clique of professional "mass organizers" in the district towns.

The less the value of the labour-day, the more important to the farmer is his household plot. It is only in a very small proportion of the farms that the labour-day is of sufficient value, and enough labour-days are earned, for the household plot to be unimportant in the standard of living. In far more of the farms it is in effect the only source of the farmer's income: these are the farms in which the collective work normally provides only for the obligatory off-farm product and for seed and fodder. In such farms the maximum time and effort is naturally put into the private acre and animals, which their holders try to increase beyond the legal maximum. The government has several times attempted to check these increases, especially in the size of plot, and has enacted that every member of a collective farm must take part in the collective work, at least to the extent of earning a certain number of labour-days at each season. This legally compulsory minimum ranges from 100 to 150 labour-days a year per member, and this applies to the women as well as the men. The amount of actual working time spent over a year to earn 150 labour days will, of course, vary from more than 150 actual days to less according to skill and responsibility. It is not likely to exceed 200 actual days for any adult. These laws have remained official ideals in many farms, but they were not relaxed in the reforms of 1953; in fact, the big tax reductions on household plots made in 1953 do not apply to families in which the collective work minimum is not performed by any member of the family.[1]

Those families which have had to make a living off their private plots have had a very thin time, for their acre and animals have had to provide heavy off-farm supplies as compulsory deliveries (like the collective sector) and in addition heavy money taxes on the "assessed value" of vegetable, meat, milk and other production, which normally forced the family to sell part of its produce in the town markets and some of its young animals to the collective farm so as to get the money to pay taxes. About the time of amalgamation, the government began to raise these taxes so high that it was becoming unprofitable to own a cow, and millions were sold off the private plots to join the collective herds or for meat. (Previously, more than half the cows in the country had been privately owned.) The last turn of the screw was in January 1953, and it looks as if the policy being followed was one of driving the

---

[1] In the summer of 1954 an important change was announced. Each farm now decides for itself the minimum of labour-days to be put into its collective work by its members, and those members not reaching this minimum are still penalized by heavier taxes on their private plots. The farms are asked by the government to set minima high enough to ensure completion of all their planned collective work; and they appear to be raising the number for men but not for women, and excusing mothers of small children. The minima for men can be set much higher than before because, with the new higher returns from the state for their grain, meat and other produce, the majority of farms can now ensure for their members the main part of their livelihood from the collective work. The importance of the change is that it shifts the weight of the struggle between collective and individualistic ways of work from a struggle between the state and the farms to a struggle within every farm. The change also means much more self-government by the farms which fulfil their plans.

farmers off the private plot into complete dependence on the collective work, but the result may have been more in the direction of undermining the collective work by the kind of passive resistance in which the villagers of the old Russian Empire have a long tradition. The government relaxed the pressure by the Budget of August 1953 and in September officially recognized the necessity of the private plot and cow in the farmers' standard of living.

In the period up to 1953 the chief characteristic of collective farming was reorganization of the labour force on the basis of rather small investment—though the equipment of the MTS was probably as much as industry could manage, granted the overriding purpose of industrialization and military requirements in this period. The chief result has been an increase in grain production, and especially in the off-farm movement of grain, which has ended the recurrent threat of famine and has fed the towns in their growth from a population of 30,000,000 to 80,000,000. Secondly, the peasants have been shown that they are living and working within an overall system which knows its mind, which is capable of getting the off-farm product it requires within the legal forms it lays down and whether the peasant eats or not, and which—if intelligently used by the peasant—can provide a standard of rural living beyond his dreams a generation ago. At the same time the whole process of industrialization, and the other than economic relations between town and country, have been so managed that the conflict of interest between the townsman and his country cousin when there was not enough to eat for both, instead of being allowed to drive either class into revolt or more or less abject dependence on the other, has forced the peasants out of their traditional isolationism, to consider and to enter into a highly complex and reciprocal relation with the industrial towns.

But although the bread was thus secured, variety and adequacy of diet, especially in the towns, were not. Consequently, many or most of the factories and other urban places of work supplied their canteens with vegetables, meat and milk from their own farms. In addition many urban workers, especially in the smaller towns and new industrial centres, have large

D

allotments, and about a million of them before the war had their own cow—thus even industrialization has not proved wrong the old Russian proverb "let a woman into Paradise and she'll bring her cow". Advice and technical help to urban allotment holders is a principal part of the work of the trade unions. These two urban forms of self help in food were most obviously valuable during the war, but they have been necessary all through, and of course have kept the townsman in practical touch with some of his country cousin's problems: for example, the urban allotments are also subject to compulsory deliveries as well as to the weather.

The "state farms" were started as grain farms; and the government had great hopes of getting a large proportion from them of the bread for industrialization. The part they have played in this is important, but they were affected by the general low level of managerial competence and of capital investment in Russian agriculture before the war. Nowadays, "state farms" are owned by many Ministries, and have a variety of functions: some are run by factories and large offices for their canteens, some are experimental and scientific centres of cattle breeding and mechanization, but most are still "grain factories". Their efficiency varies widely, but on the whole is much below the expectations of the late 1920s. Their workers are paid in wages, not in labour-days, and are members of trade unions; their managers are officials of the owning Ministry.

This is the same form of organization as in industry. A Russian factory, mine or railway looks of course much the same as factories, mines or railways elsewhere; the technological division into shops and departments is naturally also very similar. The differences are on the human side. The corporate life of the factory is expressed in its production meetings, which are similar both in organization and purpose to the "Sunday Soviets" which were held in some of our Ministry of Aircraft Production factories during the war; but in Russia they are a regular and permanent feature of industrial life. The production meeting of a large factory is summoned, in or out of working hours, by the manager who usually invites the foremen and key technicians, people from the costing section of the accounts department and from the planning office, his assistant managers on the technical, labour and financial sides, and the *"aktiv"* amongst the workers. This *aktiv* has no formal definition: in practice it differs slightly from meeting to meeting according to the particular weak spots in production or efficiency that are to be discussed; its members become members by virtue of experience, seniority, knowledgeability, influence among their fellows, ability to express themselves clearly, drive and gumption—in general, for their usefulness to the purpose of the meeting. The *aktiv*, like the other people at the meeting, are invited by the manager, but in selecting them he normally consults the party branch secretary and perhaps the trade union secretary too: and both of these officials, with their immediate assistants, usually of course attend the meeting. The production meetings do not decide policy in any broad sense whatever: that is already laid down in the plan. Their purpose is to analyse weak places in production as compared with the plan, which in practice means in the main questions of output, production costs and quality. These of course lead into all the ordinary problems of production anywhere in conditions of full employment: how to make up for shortage of supplies in some line, what to do about absenteeism, wastages, proportion of rejects, how the new workers are coming on and how the older workers present can speed up their learning, the performance of a new machine in the opinion of the technician, foreman and one or two of the men working on it, rate-fixing anomalies that may be affecting output. The canteen manager and perhaps a cook and waitress will be present as well as the convenor of the canteen sub-committee of the trade union if the canteen service is on the agenda. The frequency of the meetings depends on the personalities, habits and business relationships of the manager and party secretary, the occurrence and kinds of production crises, the general level of factory morale and the effectiveness of the trade union on the production side. Thus, meetings may be held regularly (for instance, once a month); or only in times of production crisis—and then often; or merely as a matter of form once or twice a year under managers of a certain type. There are no formal regulations or standing orders to govern or regulate these meetings; and where they are properly used their informality is perhaps the most effective and valuable thing about them.

Meetings called by the trade union in a factory (apart from its own committee, etc., meetings) are of three kinds, which we can call works meetings and shop meetings, and "public" meetings of the workers as citizens. The Russian trade unions are industrial unions and one union ordinarily comprises the workers of all kinds, from cleaners to managers, employed by one industrial Ministry. (The kind of exception is shown by the canteen workers who in most industries belong to the Trade Union of Catering Workers: but the cleaners in the factories belong to their industrial union.) Thus there is only one union of railway employees, and though this union has at various times been split into several unions by area because of the size of the country, there is among the railway employees no conflict between different unions or different principles of unionism, but workers on light railways belonging to a factory or mine are members of their industrial union. The number of unions in the engineering industry has increased roughly in accordance with the development of technological specialization and the size of the industry. The number of Ministries or departments of Ministries has also tended to multiply for the same reason, and the people employed by one of the smaller Ministries or by a department of a larger Ministry normally have their own union. The parallelism is not mechanical, and the trade union structure does not follow every shift of the administrative structure. But since both structures are young they are both flexible, and there is a close general correspondence between them. Russian trade unionism has thus developed, in an industrializing period, a mode of structure and of structural change calculated not to tie trade unions to particular technological stages in productive technique or to involve them in demarcation and other inter-union disputes; they have the simpler method of transferring a man from one union to another if he moves from one industry to another. The factory works manager is in his industrial union, the manager's own boss at the Trust or Ministry office is in the Civil Service Union—which will also include the boss's office cleaner. This mode of trade union organization helps to give the works, shop or "public" meetings convened by the union at the place of work the singleness of background and conduct which forms the climate of these meetings.

At the shop level, the trade union's main concerns are the problems of a newly skilled working class at the detailed point of production: skill and its applications, the use of wage-rates and their differentials, and rivalry in various forms with other shops. The increase of skill and improvement of organization at the point of production are the main interest of the trade unions, and there are many devices for fostering its application, for example, real costing (of labour, materials, power and repairs per unit output) by the workers on each similar machine in a shop, and analysis of the differences "to bring up the backward to the average" and "bring up the average to the best"; and competition between shops of the same factory or of different factories for the thoroughness of real costing methods (such workers' costing is independent of, though normally it receives much help from, the managerial cost accounting done by the factory accounts department). Workers' own costing—which itself takes many forms—is only one of a very large number of devices for increasing efficiency; new ones are always being thought of, and their inventors become famous to the newspaper readers for a few weeks. These devices are often lumped together under the names "Stakhano-vite movement" and "socialist competition", and these are the chief subjects of shop trade union meetings. "Socialist competi-tion" in a narrower sense means highly organized contests between factories for Challenge Banners awarded by civic authorities, the trade unions, the Ministries, Republic govern-ments or the national government. Adjudication in these competitions is based on percentage of real and money cost reduction. Money prizes go with the Banners, the current holders of which proudly display them in the factory club or the manager's office.

Wage-rates and their differentials are not negotiated in the shops: it is their application which is discussed there. A man's wage-rate depends on his grading, and this is determined (whether he is a new worker or an applicant for up-grading) by an official test of skill conducted by a Grading Commission. This consists of senior workers and, in important cases, foremen and technicians as well, all delegated by the management. Demotion from a grade by the management must have the agreement of the trade union; otherwise the case is taken to a Rates and Conflicts Commission, on which the management and trade union are equally represented, and to which workers bring appeals against decisions by foremen or managers about their grading, movement to other work or suspension, or complaints about conditions of work. These Commissions are organized at shop or shift level, and therefore normally are very knowledgeable and quick in coming to decisions. If the two sides of the Commission are not in agreement, the case goes to the Labour Division of the local People's Court.

The backbone of the trade union at shop level is the shop steward, who sees not only to dues collection and membership but also to all the activities of the trade union amongst the group of up to twenty workers for whom he acts. The Shop Committee consists of some of the shop stewards and other workers, possibly including one or two foremen; it is elected by the shop but is under the general authority of the Factory Trade Union Committee.

The routine work of an ordinary trade union branch covering a whole factory is complex and many-sided and has shown considerable historical development. In the industrializing period, especially during its early years, and in the war, one of the main functions of the trade union branch was to ensure its members' food supplies, and for this purpose it had a number of means whose proportionate importance has varied with the difficulties of the times. The branch elects Food Inspectors who have considerable powers, including that of dismissing grocery shop assistants and managers: their activity and use of their powers vary according to the locality and food supply situation —in difficult times they control (on behalf of the branch and under the instructions of its committee) the entire handling and allocation of food through the works canteens and local shops serving the factory area; in easier times they are more concerned with cleanliness and civility. This side of trade union power cannot, from its very nature, be exactly and neatly defined:

it depends on the tension and solidarity embodied in the branch, the forcefulness and effectiveness of the branch organization and leadership: in easy times its work may be quite unobtrusive, in difficult times it may be the virtual dictator over everybody concerned in the local food supply organizations, especially where there is a clearly defined population group associated with a particular factory or mine.

The powers of a trade union branch over the local housing —including construction, allocation and maintenance—can be, in appropriate circumstances, just as great. Almost all the new housing built during the industrialization has been built by industries to house their own workers, including barracks mainly for single young workers as well as tenement blocks for families. The housing put up for or by a factory at the expense of the Ministry or Trust is under the factory manager's control, but where the trade union branch is strong in relation to the manager, or works in effective co-operation with him, it supervises the plans and construction work, allocates the new dwellings, takes charge of the barracks, controls repairs, and has a decisive voice in the allocation of certain factory funds which can be used for new housing or other purposes. The statutory powers of the trade unions in housing (which are less than in food) are less important than "the custom of the works", which is a product of the past effectiveness of the branch in this and similar matters. With recent and prospective improvements in food supplies the point of sharpest stringency, and therefore of trade union struggle and effort on the supply side, is now housing.

By contrast with these sides of welfare which are the necessary preoccupations of trade union power during an industrialization, the sides of welfare which are familiar to us as the aims of trade union power after industrialization —factory medical services, creches in areas of female labour, factory clubs, etc.—are relatively available, without any sustained and hard struggle for them, as recognized rights of the industrial working class. They come within the sphere of trade union attention and effort as questions of enlargement of scope and improvement of quality and as the business of their administration, for they have been run by the unions since the Commissariat of Labour was dissolved in 1933 and its functions handed over to the T.U.C.

Inside the factory the branch is concerned both with the corporate life of the factory and with certain special aspects, such as administering sickness and disability benefits, appointing, and providing of information to, the Factory Inspectors (who are trade union officers, but on government pay). Another special aspect is provided by the workers' inventions and "rationalization" movement: it is of course the management's responsibility to examine and use or reject these ideas, but there is a branch sub-committee which in many works keeps a sharp eye on the management because of the pressure by the inventors and rationalizers, who stand to gain a percentage of the savings made if an idea is used. I once met a small and diffident engineer looking for a new job; he was in charge of the preliminary examination of workers' ideas at a big works in Gorky, and had to turn down several thousand useless ones each year to prevent them cluttering up the higher channels. The righteous indignation of their muscular authors, with powerful backing from the union for many of them, was making his life too unquiet as a buffer between the men and the management.

All the legally recognized kinds of interactions of the men and management are stated in the Collective Agreement negotiated annually in detail by the trade union branch along general lines agreed between the union national executive and the Ministry. These agreements are long documents, usually issued to each worker as a printed booklet when confirmed. They include wage rates in detail, but only for information, as the branch is not supposed in the eyes of the law to play any part whatsoever in negotiating wages. The negotiated parts of the agreement fall under two headings: "Obligations Undertaken by the Management" and "Obligations Undertaken by the Workers". Wage negotiations, where they occur, are illegal arrangements, not written down in the agreement, for example that a certain number of men be up-graded. If the number is so large that the manager's wages fund will be substantially exceeded by up-grading, he will in return get the trade union to promise improved output, as most managers are—or were before the war—usually on the point of being strangled by their wages bills, and the banks do not give credit for long to a factory whose costs exceed incomings. So the negotiators of the trade union branch do their best as go-betweens to keep wage discontents within limits. A strong branch can make a manager spend more money on housing and amenities than is earmarked by higher authority. In addition, there is a "Manager's Fund" disposable by agreement between manager and trade union, which is normally small but rises steeply if the factory has a good year, and an effective union branch can get most of this for workers' bonuses, workers' housing and so forth, while in factories where the union is ineffective most of this fund is more likely to go into production purposes and as bonuses for managerial and technical staffs. (The Manager's Fund is up to 4 per cent of cost reductions that were planned and up to 50 per cent of cost reductions in excess of plan.)

It is on all these matters of output, skill, grading, food supply, housing and the rest, that trade union shop and factory meetings are held. What I have called the trade union "public" meetings are those convened on national political occasions, such as the arrest of Beria in July 1953 and his execution in December, and the troubles in Eastern Germany in June 1953. On such occasions the party circularizes all its branches throughout the country to convene, mainly through the trade unions, mass meetings of all workers at their places of work, to condemn, express sympathy or praise as the case may be. Without exception, such "public" political meetings proceed, after reiterations of the key phrases from the *Pravda* editorial on the subject, to statements of what is to be done about the event in question, and always this is stated in terms of better work, over-fulfilment of plan in a good factory or fulfilment in a bad one, as the practical expression of the feeling voiced at the meeting. A small enough shop meeting of this kind will spend most of its time on fairly detailed discussion of how to improve production. This immediate turning of tears of anger, sorrow or joy into sweat does not, of course, appear much in the newspaper reports of the meetings, which therefore sound childish and unreal outside Russia; but it is much the most important result of a meeting for the people who are actually at it. Moreover, the upsurge or downswing of actual material production in industry after such a wave of meetings gives the political authorities fairly sound evidence of whether the industrial workers are with them or not at the time: it is a sensitive barometer of public mood and feeling which is by convention entrusted to the trade unions for their handling.

In the years 1928–52 Russia was not only industrializing but doing so very fast and without capitalists. The place of the entrepreneur was taken by the factory or works manager, who resembles his capitalist counterpart in several respects, though the forms of organization in which he operates are very different. The manager is of course a servant of the state, appointed by his Ministry and solely responsible to the Ministry for the works and its plan fulfilment. He has had to be capable of getting more out of his workers than any capitalist entrepreneur, and of conjuring supplies out of the greatest sellers' market known to history. He has had to be able to keep two powerful or potentially powerful organizations (the party branch and the trade union branch, each with its own characteristic driving forces and understanding of the production effort) if not in double harness then at least on the same road. He has had to be brazen, diplomatic, threatening and cringing as occasion required to the local branch of the State Bank, to the technicians, politicians and organizers at the Ministry, to the legal authorities and to the political police. Nor has he, typically, failed to supplement a salary that may be reasonable to the eyes of an artless observer but which is a wholly inadequate reward for so forceful a compound of energetic virtues and effective vices, by seizing in passing such perquisites of his office, whether legal or just available, as came his way. He is the alternative and near kinsman to the Russian ex-peasant capitalist, and in the public mind he is regarded with the deepest suspicion and the greatest awe. He, and not the intellectual, is the Russian "middle class"; when the Russian intellectuals (inside and outside politics) disputed this, they were purged and he was the purger. He is not unlettered, but he has no sophisticated fear of a cliché; he is enterprising, but the good things of life are for him not entirely confined to material success;

his training has been among men and machines, not in the money market. For all his hard-earned worldly wisdom, he has still somewhere about him a touch of innocence which both keeps him a man of the people, and confounds his adversaries the more, the greater the measure of their own cunning.

As has been said, it is at provincial level that industry and agriculture meet. The senior secretary of a Province party committee is the most direct and immediate boss of the bigger works managers in his area: he has to be all they are and more. That is why these offices, and those above them in Moscow, have never been filled by routine or career appointments. The men for these jobs have to be handpicked, and are. Stalin's personal authority was, to the Russian people, accounted for by the fact that he was also a product of the forces which produced these men, that he governed them with an iron hand, and that he yoked the weight and direction of their untempered strength with the diffuser and gentler but no less persistent vigour of ordinary people in an unsophisticated land. The entry into Middle Socialism had to wait for, among other things, the cutting of these originally extremely rough diamonds into preciser industrial uses, so that with such precision there could come also some degree of stable specialization of social function and status.

In addition to the inside of his factory, the manager is responsible for all its external relations. On the business side these are normally summed up in The Plan, but this is by no means so simple as it sounds. Planning, as it developed in Early Soviet Socialism, was born on the political side of the revolutionary movement and combined a number of sources— the working class's necessity (following on the revolution and civil war) to run industrialization itself, the very practical ideas of technical people like Grinevetsky, the tradition of the state as industrialist. All these ideas were combined in the minds of the political people, who themselves varied very much in practicality and understanding of what was feasible: there were very few men with engineering or business experience amongst them, but many fluent romantics. There were also a large number of enthusiastic statisticians, for in Tsarist Russia the more respectable progressives found an outlet in studying social trends, as an alternative to illegal political activity. After the revolution these were organized in and around the Supreme Council of National Economy and its local sections, in the State Planning Commission, and so forth. The early history of such institutions typically falls into these periods: realization of the actual condition of the country or industry; division into conservative and romantic wings with opposing policies; employment of members of these wings both in their public and private capacities by different groups of politicians in the party debates; defeat of one side in these debates and defeat of its wing of experts in the planning institution (such defeats being accompanied by arrests, suicides, and executions when industrialization started); fission of the victorious wing into new conservative and romantic elements, and so on. This whole process was by no means so chaotic as it sounds. It was, so to speak, a normal process which went abnormally fast and with an unusual verbosity and, at critical times, mortality. Out of it all there came the successive drafts of the first five-year plan which in its final draft was two plans side by side called the optimal and minimal variants: it was ratified in its optimal version, which was the politicians' and planners' forecast of what could be done if there was good weather for the crops and favourable terms of trade for imports. We have already seen that in actually fulfilling this plan whole sections of it had in practice to be abandoned while others were carried right through and over the crisis, far in advance of what was planned, and that the process in fact made new men more quickly than it made new machines.

The experience of putting through the first plan was reflected in both the realistic and romantic elements in the second plan. This was adopted as a unified plan without variants; its romantic element lay in a tendency to encourage over-large production units where these were neither necessary nor desirable and at the same time aim at a standard of living which was visionary even without these giant investments. In spite of these features, however, the second plan was far more orderly than the first and so there began to be established a routine of its administration, the general lines of which are still followed.

The plan as adopted by the government is broken down in two ways, by time and by factories, so that when a works manager gets his plan from his Ministry what he gets is a plan for the year divided into quarterly target figures. When the plan arrives it rarely holds any real surprises: the manager already has his five-year plan (in which investment in his factory and its productivity trends are most prominent), and he also has for several months been telling his Ministry what he can be expected to do over the plan year on the resources it offers him. In the ordinary way, therefore, the arrival of the plan is simply a formal confirmation of his worst fears, for which he has already made some provision. These up-and-down channels of administration were in the main established during the second five-year plan, and it was also during that period that the managers and others began to establish a criss-cross network of formal relationships amongst themselves which soon extended upward to involve the Trusts and Ministries.

A factory does not of course deliver its products to its Ministry; it has its customers, whose production or sales or construction programmes are dependent on the supplies they are expecting. The works manager's annual plan provides for his main supplies and deliveries, but not in detail. All such details as delivery dates are dealt with in the contracts he makes with his suppliers and customers. It happens as often in Russia as elsewhere that agreement on a contract is not easily reached or that a contract is not fulfilled, and these problems have to be dealt with even though all the managers concerned are the servants of a single administrator—the state. This is where the lawyers come in. They have erected an elaborate system of State Arbitration, which settles conflicts over contracts before as well as after they are signed by the managers. The contracts must be made, as they are the necessary criss-cross interlacing of all the up-and-down administered plans, so that arguments in the State Arbitration Courts over failure to *sign* a contract are as important as the arguments over failure to *fulfil* a contract. The State Arbitration Courts have the power to decide the terms and clauses of a contract disputed before signature, as well as the terms of compensation, etc., for failure to fulfil a contract where the liability or the penalties contained in the contract itself are disputed. A large proportion of cases of both kinds are settled out of court, through *de facto* arbitration carried out by the lawyers on both sides. (It was a pleasing sight before the war to see a prim pre-revolutionary lawyer telling two proletarian types at loggerheads that they ought to settle out of court since they were both servants of the Soviet state and the Arbitration Court was busy.)

The life of a business lawyer working for a Russian factory or trust is not confined to his highly respectable and useful duties in arbitration practice, or appearing for the management at the Labour Division of the People's Court. His more wearing experiences occur when he has to protect his manager from the consequences of circumventing shortages of supply. For this single purpose the manager employs a subordinate crony who, whatever his formal title in the factory's establishment list, has as his main qualification that of expert scrounger. During industrialization there has been an appalling shortage of almost every kind of industrial supply, and in many cases it was due to these procurements men that factories kept running at all. By the end of the second five-year plan the position was becoming more regular in various ways: the industrial supply situation was easing in spite of the government's continuing pressure on productive capacity; planning was every year becoming more experienced and provident; to some extent the activities of the managers' cronies were becoming canalized and legalized; and, most important of all, the new managerial group had broken its rivals within the party fellowship in the great purge and had established its own new fraternity. In a sense the party now became "monolithic" for the first time: whether from the newly skilled working class, the new technical and managerial strata, the newly collectivized peasantry or the top leadership, the members now had a common practicality which had driven out and destroyed the fluent romanticism that had been so striking a feature of the previous period. The new membership had, as they say, a common language, and consequently was able to supplement all the formal intercommunication of a modern economy by those reliable oral agreements and quick personal communications without which no industry can in fact work.

An increasingly stringent side of a works manager's external affairs is in his relations with his bank. The investment funds allocated to him come through the Industrial Bank, which—if there is construction work on a fairly big scale going on—will have a man on the spot checking the expenditure of these funds, for they neither bear interest nor are returnable. The work's current account is with the local branch of the State Bank, which is a long-suffering but orthodox institution. Many a factory manager has resorted to such devices as arrangements with local shops to borrow their takings for paying wages when, owing to delays in the factory's deliveries, payments to the factory by its customers were late and the bank was refusing further accommodation. More factories in the Russian than in capitalist economies ran on financial shoe-strings in the later 1930s when "control by the ruble" was becoming a reality but supplies and transport were not yet regular enough to let the financial control work smoothly. Current Russian textbooks for bankers and accountants show in great detail the interdependence of the production and the financial plans and the workings of financial controls; their authors assume for purposes of exposition that these arrangements are as automatically effective as they are painstakingly ingenious. The Russian works manager, however, not having to waste his ingenuity on his income tax, has more to spare on his financial plan. This is why it is formally laid down by law that a works accountant must both obey any order given by his manager and, at the same time, inform the Trust or Ministry of irregularities. (There is no profession of independent accountants in Russia. "Outside" checking of a factory's books is done by officials of the Ministry of Finance, and the Ministry of State Control which in 1933 replaced the meddlesome and often very ignorant Workers' and Peasants' Inspectorate.)

One of the most important sides of the plan as received by a works manager is in its productivity figures, but in coping with these problems the manager does not stand alone. He and his technicians are simply one special group within the factory community as a whole, and it is as a member of this

community whose consciousness of its unity is expressed in
the trade union branch, that the manager addresses himself
to the problems which are set for him by the productivity figures
in the plan. These figures are part of the year's plan of material
output, but they express that output in terms of human efficiency in handling materials and machines: and it is in this sense
that productivity is "planned". Government policy has been
throughout industrialization, and still is, to get these figures
set each year in every factory sufficiently higher than the
previous year to make the manager and everyone else in the
factory scour deep in organizing and doing the work better
than before.

What is called "discovering reserves" consists in examining
the organization of the work teams, the effectiveness of the
machinery, the layout of the production system, etc., to find
where effort or resources are running to waste, and turning them
into productive channels. In the early days of industrialization
the amount of slack that could be taken up in various places was
sometimes enormous. For example, in preparing the plan for
1936, *on known resources* the planners proposed an output of
30,000 railway wagons, which were at that time one of the key
shortages in the economy. The government told the planners to
find hidden resources for the output of an extra 50,000 wagons.
The technical and organizational search revealed amongst
other things that work in the river ship repair yards was very
slack for a whole season each year, so their equipment and
labour force were turned on to making wagons. By this and
similar means nearly all the extra 50,000 were made, with
relatively little disturbance to the rest of the plan. Nowadays
the taking in of slack is a much less spectacular matter and also
much more continuous: the continual creep of technological
progress is of itself always creating small pockets of unused
resources, and a community which keeps a sharp eye open for
this sort of thing can save years in the advance to a general
prosperity. Consequently the key figures of the national plan are
considered by the government partly from the point of view
of how far any stepping up of them will lead to better organization and the quicker discovery of hidden resources. This
probing know-how had already before the war gone so far that

the alteration of the figure for the increase in productivity for an industrial Ministry from, say, 6.3 per cent to 6.5 per cent by the government at a late stage in the compilation of the plan would keep people in the State Planning Commission, the Ministry and its factories up for nights on end making the consequential readjustments throughout the plan and thereby "searching out unused resources".

By far the most important unused, or rather, insufficiently used resource is labour, since more of it can always become more skilled and in fact has to, because industrial production consists of a flow, tardy or rapid, of new machines and methods. In Russia this flow is very rapid, while the working class is newly skilled, so that awareness of this unused resource is very keen. The Russian wages system is designed to promote skill in the handling and mastery of new machines and in the improvement of organization at the point of production.

In the national annual plan there is a Wages Fund for all employees. This is also (with certain adjustments) the money expression of that part of the consumable national wealth which is expected to be available for sale. Any modern industrial economy produces for three purposes: (1) investment and stocks, (2) defence, and (3) consumption. (Exports may serve any of these purposes; during Early Socialism Russia used exports to import goods necessary for investment, but is now beginning to import goods for consumption.) The Russian economy differs from its contemporaries in that the government decides, and decides in real and not financial terms, what changes there shall be in the proportions of the national wealth dedicated to each purpose. The largest decisions settle the main flows of wealth for half a generation at a time, for example the decision to industrialize directed the main flow into capital investment for fifteen years, a period of "everything for basic industry" which was broken by the war (when it was "everything for the front") and extended by the consequences of the war to 1952. As a matter of fact, because of the shifting and conversion of industry during the war, the period of Early Soviet Socialism ended with a more widespread and more up-to-date industry than had been envisaged as resulting from the direction of the first main flow. At the end of the 1930s

E

the planners were working on the preparation of a second
fifteen-year plan for splitting the main flow so as to bring consumption up to compatibility with the new production level.
Instead, because of the war, the main flow into investment and
defence continued and the contrast between production and
consumption increased, so the solution imposed by this ac-
centuated contrast was a different one: the change in the
direction of the main flow in 1953 consisted partly in shifting
the proportions between investment and consumption and partly
in dividing the investment stream to begin the thorough
capitalization of agriculture. This means, so far as we can tell,
that it will be only when this new stage of investment in agriculture is completed that a further basic shift in the proportions
of investment and consumption will be possible, and it is likely
that this will first become apparent in the form either of a
housing programme or of the construction of new consumer
goods industries. (The only such industries there are now
are textiles, footwear and food-processing; other things are still,
even after the improvements of 1953, produced in the holes
and corners of the economy: either in small, poorly equipped
factories and workshops run by their workers as producers'
co-operatives or by the local authority, or in odd parts of big
engineering works, to a great extent on scrap materials.)

It is within these largest decisions that the policy aims of
each five-year plan are laid down. Within the first half-
generation, for example, the three five-year plans were for
the establishment of the key heavy industrial branches of a
modern economy (1928–32), for the equipping of these branches
with machinery and skill (1933–37) and for the completion
of this process and establishment of the remaining branches of
heavy industry (1938–42). These were the strategic forced
marches within the overall deployment of resources; it was at
the turning point of the overall deployment, in 1936, that the
"entry into socialism" was formally made by the adoption of a
new constitution. This constitution opened perspectives of
development extending far beyond the first half-generation.

The achievement of a constitution with a reasonable
expectation of life had been a Russian aim for several generations. The passion for a written constitution was a natural

outcome of three centuries of lawless government: the nature of the new constitution was, however, widely misunderstood outside Russia. Granted that an unwritten constitution is by far the best kind to have, Russian people with their history could not be satisfied with anything but a written one. Among written constitutions the worst are those which are true at the time they are adopted, for the wear and tear of time will soon make them untrue and they will strangle instead of spur on the development of public affairs. The Russian constitution makers seem to have been the first people to observe that among written constitutions the best is that which is not yet true at the time it is adopted, so that its expectation of life will be real and it will be a constant model and stimulus, a proper repository for the idealism of a growing community, a criterion whereby it can measure its progress towards what it regards as the proper management of its affairs. So the adoption of the new constitution in 1936 served to mark the Russian certainty that they had broken with the past and set their feet on a new road, and that they had the resources within themselves to follow that road to its end.

We have already seen that new men came out of the industrialization and that some of them took the places in the economy and society which had previously been held by technicians of the old Russian sort and the more fluent and romantic kind of politician. The Russian intellectual and white collar worker had, apart from some exceptional individuals, the kind of attitude to his own common people which is only paralleled in this country by the attitude of people who weep for the sorrows and shortcomings of their black brethren but uphold the colour bar. In addition, the resulting hothouse atmosphere within which the intellectuals conversed with one another produced a belief in the power of pure words (the more abstract the better) which was only matched by their ignorance of the ways of ordinary life. As a result, those among the common people who were coming up to the economic and social place previously occupied by these delicate enthusiastic plants felt the full brunt and insult of this ignorance, empty verbosity and ecstatic chattering arrogance. The process of the long desired industrialization, its enlargement and bracing

by the new constitution, the vigour imparted by the sense of
seeing a way through, and the first touch of the long cold
shadows of the coming war, together gave the edge of exaspera-
tion to the great purge of 1936–38 that ended in the eyes of the
commoners the last survivals of gentry-mindedness in the
superior avocations.

Many of the people purged had a long and honourable
revolutionary career behind them, but this did not count if it
was marked by the fatal touch of patronage. Many others were
just entering upon useful careers; this also did not count if
they were or were believed to be carriers of the intolerable
taint. Many had done no more than follow without thinking
the slight extravagances of life of their friends and associates.
Perhaps most of them had barked their alarm about the betrayal
of the revolution, the "Thermidorian Reaction" or the failure
of the state to wither away, far more loudly than anyone
imagined they could ever bite. But whether they were hardened
or innocent, or merely harmless and negligible, they were swept
up in a final determination to be shut once and for all of everything that no longer had to be tolerated from the politicians
of the revolution. By 1936 the Russian commoners were out to
cure their world and they were no longer in a mood to continue
their immemorial endurance. It was a day of reckoning,
when the people who thought they had made the revolution
found their occupation gone and their credit exhausted with
the people whose revolution it was and whose one desire was to
achieve the prosperous and powerful stability then at last in
sight.

So great a source of upheaval could not fail to have reper-
cussions on the economic development, particularly as the
administrative and industrial officials were the occupations
most affected. But it imposed a delay rather than a difference
in development. The rising social force of the new highly
skilled tradesmen, the new technicians (trained since the
beginning of industrialization and who had in part been skilled
workmen before), and the works managers of the new type,
was strong enough not only to oust its rivals from the posts
they held on the strength of their revolutionary services, but
also to take up their work in the economic structure and social

fabric with a remarkably short pause in the general stride of the country's business. These new people had been making their way in the world in social status and authority, and at the same time had been establishing the wage differentials of that wide range which still startles foreign visitors to Russia.

The old traditions of the revolutionary movement had been egalitarian, and this was reinforced both by the equalizing sharing out of the landowners' fields amongst the peasants in 1917–18 and by the equalizing effect of poverty in the towns during the civil war, when there were pieces of bread for wages. The hangover of this *political* tradition was weakened in the first five-year plan, when industrialization began to impose its own new needs on old ideas, and was destroyed in the purge whose driving force was those groups which were making their way in the world in more senses than one. The *social* roots of egalitarianism were, however, something quite different: they lay in the countryside, and the industrializing working class was rapidly and continuously growing by immigration from the countryside. The immigrants brought with them into the factories modes of organization long traditional in the rural depths and the old industry of Russia. The most familiar of these was for several men from a village to organize themselves into an artel, a sort of club or unskilled labour gang, and go off together to seek their joint fortunes in a town, to find industrial employment together, to pool their earnings and divide them out equally or according to need. In old Russia, this was the form of organization out of which there grew the ex-peasant capitalist who became, from the leader of such an artel, its exploiter, and raised himself by hiring other artels. The artels of rural immigrants were, up to the war, still coming into Russian industry, where they were a real headache for the trade unions and managements: here in real life were the potential seeds of the most vicious type of capitalism, and here also in the same phenomenon was the foreshadowing of the principle towards which the working class is so eagerly moving, distribution according to needs. (This egalitarian aspect of the artel tradition has been confused, by foreign observers, with the "fair shares" of the welfare state: actually it bears the same kind of relationship to the ethics of the welfare state as the democracy of a tribal pow-wow bears to the democracy of representative government.)

Of course neither trade unions nor management could do anything if such an artel did pool its pay-packets: what they could do was to try and assign the members of an artel to different work teams in a factory, though the men might not stay on under these conditions and labour was always in short supply. Another manifestation of the same tradition was the practice in some factories of paying the wages of a work team in a single pay-packet which, in the context of artel traditions still surviving within modern industry, was often divided equally or more or less according to need.

In brief, the development of wage differentials during the 1930s marked the coming to predominance of a specifically industrial working class now independent both of the intellectuals' political tutelage and of its own origins in the countryside.

At the same time as wage differentials were increased, bonus systems were sharpened to make the prospect of attaining the extra bit of skill and output as attractive as possible. The entry of a man into the higher grades of skill classification or into the higher rewards of a bonus system usually marked the turning point in his process of breaking with the old ties and traditions. By no means all who were capable of earning the new wages were willing to pay this price for them, and the resentments at the people who did break away were sometimes bitter enough to lead to murder. Even within the older established industrial labour force, technology had been stagnant for nearly twenty years, so that recapitalization and reorganization led to the breaking up of many comfortable and established ways of doing things. The tensions in such circumstances could be very great, as may be measured by the existence of a regulation that a man whose rationalization suggestion has caused a cut in the pay per unit output is himself exempt from this cut for a period of six months. What was being broken up by the application of such regulations was not the kind of cohesion that there is amongst industrial workers of the sixth or eighth generation, but the bonds and traditions either of a pre-industrial or of a manufactory stage of production. Seeing these stresses and strains in a contemporary industrialization should make the working class of a fully industrialized country less complacent about its own origins, about the catastrophes to old worlds of living from which people were torn and the brutalities of new worlds into which they were flung, about how they at first turned all this inwards against each other and how they came, through generations of slow understanding, to turn it all with equal force into a working-class solidarity. Industrialization in Britain, for instance, is marked by a history of organized rioting and machine-wrecking over at least a hundred and fifty years, up to the 1860s when bombs were being put down the chimneys, and gunpowder in the machines, of outworker cutlers in Sheffield. The Russian industrialization saw plenty of wrecking which expressed both workers' grievances and political opposition, and in general the maintaining of law and order amongst the social forces in the Russian industrialization was by no means any smaller problem than in the British. It cannot be too often said, as we have said before, that the *political* revolution, which rejected capitalist responsibility for industrialization, did not in any way diminish the size and depth of the *industrial* problems facing an industrializing working class. The political revolution merely made it possible to handle them, in the twentieth century, and in a country whose colonies were not conveniently overseas.

The wages system is of course a key part of the handling of these problems, and can be considered under (1) how the Wages Fund is arrived at in the national plan and how it in practice is kept at or diverges from the planned figure; and (2) how each works gets its Wages Fund and how this is allocated between all the people employed there.

Russian experience does not include planning to keep the national wealth at a stable level: backward movement or lack of movement has been due to war and to internal social crisis. All planning has been for advance. Thus the government decides the national annual plan in accordance with its estimates of increase in equipment, the labour force and skill. Its decisions about changes in the proportions of the plan are made *within* the general decisions covering half a generation, as steps in the manoeuvring to achieve the general aim set.

The decisions about intended changes from the current proportions are, of course, made within what is thought to be technically and politically possible, and are changed quickly enough during the planned year itself when this has to be done, as on the German invasion or the change in the temper of the people in 1953.

The national Wages Fund is the total of all wages (including salaries) for people employed by the central and local state authorities, and includes various other groups of money earners such as employees of the consumer co-operatives (which are for practical purposes of high policy, as distinct from detailed management, state organizations) and the members of industrial co-operatives of workers, who pay themselves in money. The Wages Fund also includes services provided in kind through factories and (probably) the pay and maintenance of special categories of people like the armed forces and convict labourers in so far as such maintenance is done by purchases of supplies for their consumption; it also includes money which will never reach the pay packet, such as income tax and the levy for the state loan which are deducted at source. With certain adjustments, however, the Wages Fund, plus the estimated money incomes of the peasantry, may be taken as the equivalent of purchasing power to buy the consumer goods planned to be available for sale at the prices decided or broadly controlled by the government in the same plan.

The national plan, in all its elaborate paper ramifications, is only the necessary scaffolding for the plan of each national organization which is responsible for the country's business. The industrial Ministries are the chief organizations of this kind. When the government has decided the national plan as a whole, the real planning work can begin: this is done at a number of meetings of the Economic Cabinet, which consists of the principal political and economic Ministers and a few representatives of other bodies such as the trade unions. The business of these sessions is to decide in outline the plan of each economic Ministry in turn. The two chief speakers on each such plan are normally the Minister and the head of the State Planning Committee, both of whom are members of the government. It is the latter who argues from the bird's-eye view of the national requirements, while the Minister will, on questions still un-resolved between his Ministry and the State Planners, put the Ministry's case. During the later stages of the work on preparing the national plan for the coming year (mainly November and December—the work itself begins in the late summer) the appropriate sections of the State Planning Committee will have been in continual close contact with people at the Ministry and even with its Trusts and largest factories, so there is not always much in dispute between the two bodies. What there is in dispute, however, is almost always decided by the government in favour of the State Planning Committee's recommendations, because even the most responsible Minister is run, to a greater or lesser extent, by his own departmental officials whose outlook is bound to have departmental blinkers, and even the most strong-minded Minister finds it less easy to take the national view than the heads of the State Planning Committee whose professional function it is to do just that.

The government decisions at these meetings, however, may not be quite what is wanted by the State Planners (whose own departmental disease is to have everything tidily balanced), and by the time each Ministry has its plan finally fixed, and the necessary provisions for other bodies (such as central subsidies to the local Republics) have been made, the national plan will not be quite the same as it was before these meetings began; the change is almost certain to be in the direction of still more pressure for searching out unused resources. But the national plan has by this stage served its purpose, as the frame-work within which those responsible for each portion of the economy have their targets of output and supplies, their in-takes of labour and their Wages Funds, and their limits of real costs clearly set. The framework plan still has its uses, however: its paper structure of many thousands of interconnecting figures will have to bear the exploratory brunt of all steps taken to meet the larger contingencies during the planned year, and the paper structure will thus acquire a somewhat different shape almost week by week throughout the year, although the plan as it was adopted in late December or early January may never have been legally changed until it finally passes into the archives, when the report on its degree of fulfilment is prepared by the state planners and statisticians in the early January of the following year.

A five-year plan of course has to meet many more and larger unforeseen contingencies than an annual plan, but that is in the nature of these "perspective" plans, whose function it is to provide a framework over time for the annual "operative" plans. One of the greatest discrepancies between the paper plans and reality has been the Wages Fund, more of course in the five-year than in the yearly plans. Wages actually paid out more and more exceeded the government's intentions during the industrialization: according to the second five-year plan the average wage should in 1937 have been 1,755 rubles a year but was 3,047 rubles according to the official records of that year (in fact it must have been more, because few works managers refrained from paying out illegal extra wages that were never recorded as wages, to hold or attract workers). The five-year plan of wages bore little relation to reality, and the Wages Funds in the annual plans, which tried each year to catch up with reality in this respect and hold the inflation, could not do so.

There were several reasons for the inflation, but the main one was production at any price, the largest element in the price being wages. What happened was a great wages scramble, which the government could not control though it made many efforts to do so. There was an additional reason for the runaway tendency in the Wages Fund during the first five-year plan, for the total labour force far exceeded the plan (it was 23,000,000 in 1932 instead of the 16,000,000 intended for 1932–33). During the second plan, however, the labour force grew more slowly than was intended (it was 27,000,000 in 1937, nearly 3,000,000 short of the plan), partly because the increase in productivity was greater than expected as the new machinery poured in. The wages scramble became sharper throughout the 1930s: the works managers had gone to any lengths for labour in the early part of the decade, and they went to any lengths for skilled labour in the latter part. The Wages Fund had become an established part of the annual plans by 1934, when the old Collective Agreements between managements and men were no longer permitted because they negotiated wages, and a planned Wages Fund cannot exist together with negotiated wages. The fact was, however, that skill could name its own price, and did because the demand for it was continually greater than the supply, and the people who came to possess it constituted a very powerful social force.

The elaborate central wage regulations became a chaos of innumerable differentials, bonuses and other extras decided in each factory. Figures of average wages have little meaning in such circumstances. The unskilled workers were left far behind, while the men who could master the new machines with their hands and break away from the old traditions in their heads earned several times the average wage; and they monopolized the kind of social services, such as the best of the new housing and free or subsidized holidays in the sanatoria, that made life worth while. The works managers and higher administrators who had also come up with industrialization (many of them Stakhanovites who had been given several years full-time special training on grants equal to their average earnings) formed the spearhead of this new and decisive element in the Russian scene, and gained an increasing proportion of their high real incomes from the perquisites of office. Other sections of the town population had to get by on small concessions: in 1937 a minimum wage of about 100 rubles a month was instituted; the government kept the teachers and clerks quiet on promises and occasional slight easements; doctors told me that their pay as public servants kept them in cigarettes and they lived on private practice after clinic hours; 15,000 miners in the Donbas coalfields were earning 1,500 rubles a month (a good deal more than university professors) when the average of all town earnings was about 250 rubles a month.

The wages scramble was all the keener because the planned output of manufactured consumer goods never came within sight of fulfilment. Off-farm grain, however, was procured to the planned extent, and this, together with the basic social services universally available in the towns, kept the industrialization going. The government, while trying to reduce the inflation, found in it the advantages which all governments do: the wage level of the masses cannot easily keep up with prices, and the task of creaming off production for the purposes of the state—in this case, industrialization—is thus made easier.

It was, and still remains, a principle of Soviet planning that productivity should rise faster than wages, in order to increase all the time the resources for investment. In the pre-war wages scramble this was not of course achieved in terms of money wages, but it was emphatically achieved in terms of real wages. Most of the main investment and output targets for heavy industry and the railways were achieved in the second plan, and some of them exceeded. Thus the inflation did not affect the substance of the plan, though it completely upset the financial side. Finance, however, does not matter in the way that the production, transport and use of materials and finished goods and the training of labour matter. The financial plans are important as a means of organizing all this real work, and as the principal regulator of distribution by allocating purchasing power. The inflationary wages scramble helped the government in creaming off purchasing power; the government in many other ways (such as its propaganda against egalitarianism and for differentials) represented the interests of the highly skilled workers and the competent organizers who were making their way in the world; and these two circumstances far outweighed merely administrative objections to the inflation.

During the war earnings continued to rise, but basic equality in essentials—so far as they were available—was maintained by rationing at pre-war prices, while high earnings could be spent on getting more of the same essentials (and some luxuries) that were sold by the state unrationed but at very high prices. Extra food could also be bought at very high prices from the farmers. The fortunes thus made in the countryside and kept in cash were abolished in the price and currency reforms of December 1947, when rationing was ended and a single new set of prices introduced. These were very high above the ration prices, so the lower wage levels were increased by about a third (thus somewhat reducing wage differentials); and since then prices have been cut considerably each year.

The most remarkable feature of financial and wages policy since the war, however, is the replacement of the pre-war scramble by a stabilization of the wage level, so that improvement in the standard of living comes mainly from the annual price reductions. Such a situation is of itself unique in economic

history, but there is also something remarkable in the sudden-
ness of the transition from the ferocious wages scramble to
(so far as we know) an orderly and pacific acceptance of price
cuts instead. The price cuts affect everybody, and the sudden-
ness of the transition reflects the speed with which the industrializing spearhead of the working class has become consoli-
dated, so that all the other sections have now rejoined it
to form a single modern working class conscious of its common
rather than sectional interests.

Since the output per man-hour is continuing to rise fast
throughout industry, the rate of money earnings per unit
output is evidently now being cut considerably every year.
Before the war, it was not easy to make these cuts periodically.
In fact, the difficulties of making these cuts were one cause of
the inflation. In questioning Russian workers, industrial
administrators, planners and economists before the war, I
obtained different accounts of the "norm-revisions" by
which such cuts were made. It was impossible to build up a
consistent picture, though there were parts or aspects of such a
picture in what each informant said. The reason was that
central policy and regulations had not much effect on the actual
situation in production, and that the practice in different
Ministries and works varied enormously. In some Ministries
there was a regular annual revision of general output norms and
wage rates, but the extent of their actual implementation
depended entirely on the situation in each works.

The Wages Fund of a Russian factory is allocated by its
Ministry, and will be supplied over the year to the manager
by the local bank on receipt of documents concerning degree of
plan fulfilment and acceptance of the factory's deliveries by its
customers. If output is running over the plan the factory's
wages account is increased automatically by the bank, and is
decreased if the plan is not being reached. These restrictions and
controls are, as we have seen, not so effective in practice as they
appear to be on paper. Inside the factory, the wages system turns
on the Grade List, which is compiled by the factory's Ministry
or Trust and states the basic hourly pay for each grade. The
number of grades varies from about six to twenty and every
manual worker is supposed to be placed in a grade according

to the skill, responsibility and conditions of his work. A man can request upgrading, for which he must according to the regulations undergo a test, and he can be downgraded for incompetence, but this is rare. The difference of basic pay between top and bottom grades may be three to one, but in practice hardly anybody nowadays—even juveniles—is found in the very lowest grades (unless a national revision of grades has taken place during 1954 to bring the system into line with current realities). The basic pay in these grade scales is in some industries half or less of actual earnings because there are so many bonus payments for extra output, for special economies of real costs, for length of time in the industry or factory, and extras for working in remote areas (e.g. 20 per cent extra in the Urals, where millions are employed) and cost of living bonuses in big towns. Since all these bonuses vary from Ministry to Ministry and factory to factory, according to departmental or factory peculiarities, anomalies within a single town or trade are striking and numerous. Handbooks of jobs and rates are issued by the wages department of each Ministry in association with the wages offices of the corresponding trade unions. These are usually fat volumes several years out of date, which endeavour to cover every trade, job and difficulty in the industry; they are also the official guides on allocation of men to their grades. In many factories the handbook is only consulted for cases of special interest, while rates are reached by agreement, but the Rates and Conflicts Commission can always refer to it if agreement is otherwise difficult.

For every job where this is possible a quota of output is fixed. This is important because bonuses for exceeding the quotas can be very high and three-quarters of the manual workers are on piece rates, while there is no lower limit for a man who does not reach his quota, unless this is due to a breakdown or other cause beyond his control. Usually, quotas are almost as out of date as the handbooks, and in 1953 there were still factories with nobody producing less than 150 per cent of his quota (this was quite common before the war—which is why so many relatively unskilled people were called Stakhanovites). The people who set the quotas may be rate-fixers, the foreman or one of the technical staff, and the usual method is by rule of thumb, the quotas set being a kind of bridge between the general instructions from the Ministry and the "custom of the works"—which itself varies from a powerful and brutal incentive system to a simple tug of war between the workers and the bank using the works manager as the rope.

The minority of workers on time rates can usually earn bonuses by saving fuel and materials or lessening repair times and rejects. Clerical staff are on standard pay with limited bonus opportunities, but managerial and technical staffs can make very high bonuses by shop or works over-fulfilment of plan.

For a systematic account of the regulations concerning the Russian wages system, and other aspects of industrial conditions, there is now an excellent book in English, *Wages, Prices and Social Legislation in the Soviet Union* by Lief Björk (Dobson, 1953, 199 pages, price 18*s*.), based on inquiries made during a visit with the Swedish T.U.C. to Moscow in 1949 and on reliable study of much Russian material. Mr. Björk is aware of how different the realities can be from the regulations, and limits his book to a clear exposition of the regulations together with much information on wages and prices at the time of his visit.

The governing reality in Soviet industry is the fact that there now exists a large working class which is not only employed in industry but has come to accept industrial conditions as a way of life. Of the five or six millions of manual workers employed in industry, construction and transport when the first five-year plan began, there could not have been much more than a million making up a modern working class. By the end of that plan, when the number of manual workers in these occupations was about thirteen million, the number of modern workers may have doubled, but the increase in their numbers was much less important than the deepening and definition of their industrial experience. Five years later, however, of a total number of manual workers only a few millions larger, the number comprising a modern working class must have been at least five millions. At present there are about thirty millions of manual workers in the same occupations, and there has been time and experience enough under the new conditions for perhaps twenty millions of them to be properly described as constituting, together with their families, an industrial working class.

CHAPTER V

PEOPLES AND IDEAS

(See map inside front cover)

RUSSIA has been in one way and another a unit for some seven hundred years, though during that time first the east, then the west, provided the rulers of the country, and there was a long period of political disunity in between: the capital was first at Karakorum in Mongolia, then at Peking, then at Moscow. During these seven centuries, many very different kinds of peoples and cultures have lived and fought together. The main groups are:

The Slav peoples of the west (the Great-Russians, White-Russians and Ukrainians or Little-Russians);

About a hundred Caucasian peoples (mainly the Great-Armenians, Georgians, and Azerbaijanians);

The Turkic and older Iranian peoples of Central Asia between the Caspian Sea and the Altai mountains (the Tadjiks are Iranian, the Kazakhs, Kirghiz, Uzbeks, Turkmenians are Turkic and Mongolian: peoples of the same stocks such as the Tartars and the Bashkirs also live to the north, on the banks of the Volga);

The Mongolian peoples to the east of the Altai;

The Finnish and Eskimo peoples of the north and north-west;

The Latvians, Lithuanians and Estonians on the Baltic.

These peoples were brought together in the Middle Ages by the making of the two great mediaeval trade-routes, both of which crossed the territory, but neither of which had a terminus on it. These two routes were the peninsular and the continental lines of communication of mediaeval Eurasia, and they met at several points. The peninsular route ran from Byzantium up the rivers of Russia to the Baltic, to the coastal cities of Germany and France and the eastern and southern ports of England, down the rivers of France (or through Biscay)

to the Mediterranean, and through Italy and Sicily to Byzantium. The continental circle ran from the Mediterranean
through Egypt, then by sea to India, Indo-China and China,
up the Hwang-ho from Peking, westwards through the Tien
Shan passes by way of Kashgar (or farther north between the
Tien Shan and the Altai), through Central Asia by way of
Samarkand, Bokhara and Khorezm, across the Caspian and
through the Caucasus to the Black Sea and Byzantium.
Besides joining at Byzantium, the two great routes were also
linked in the Mediterranean and in the Russian river-system:
in the Mediterranean, Venice entered into the sea-traffic
of the continental circuit and Genoa into the land-traffic
through her colony at Caffa in the Crimea; in the Russian
river system the Volga route running south-east from the
Baltic entered into the land-traffic of the continental route
by way of the Caspian Sea. Arab merchants from Central
Asia came up this route to Gotland Island in the Baltic,
where they met Anglo-Saxon merchants: by this means King
Alfred heard of the far-eastern Christians of St. Thomas and,
it is said, sent an embassy to their shrine.

These two great trade-routes have of course a very long
history, for they were gradually built up by the joining of
local trade-routes; and the local traffic must always have been
greater than the through. Both the local and long-distance
trade however had only a limited effect on the lands through
which it passed: it did not change their economies, but served to
stimulate greater production within the economies already
existing: generally speaking, it was an exchange of surplus
and luxury goods between diverse natural and handicraft
economies—the glass of Byzantium for the silk of China,
and so forth. The great effects of the accumulation of local
into long-distance trade were political and in the realm of
ideas, rather than in the economies. For example, Arab rule
at one time linked Spain with North Africa and Egypt, the
Near East and Central Asia: the golden road to Samarkand
organized the slave trade and the luxury handicrafts throughout
this area and strengthened, in consequence, both local feelings
of pride in traditional products and styles, and the sense of
the existence of a single world infinitely various in its parts.

F

Single systems of commercial law and international languages grew up and intertwined: the Tadjik Avicenna was one of the great scientists and philosophers of the Arab world; Jewish commercial law linked the Arab and northern areas and had an independent base in the Jewish state of Khazaria on the lower Volga; Byzantium and Rome introduced their different ideas of the single world, its nature and its future, to the peoples of the north. To this mediaeval trading world, there was one world and one God; but this one world was seen with different eyes by each of the inter-linked peoples and the nature of the one God was differently understood: Christianity and Islam both embraced a crowd of heresies and engendered them in one another and in Jewry, and produced sophisticated versions of the marginal heathenisms.

The organizational and political problems along the great trade-routes were concerned not with production as such, but the relating of production to trade: not with the mode of production on the farm and in handicrafts, but with getting the off-farm and handicraft products into trade, with policing the trade-routes, fixing tolls and providing toll-free areas, drawing new districts into the trading network, and developing the always delicate balance between the proportion of the off-farm product that maintained local and national governments, and the proportion of the product that went into trade. This balance was delicate economically but not politically: in out-lying areas it tended to be extracted by banditry, piracy and slave-raiding as a first stage, and then by a more orderly exac-tion of tribute. So in the north, the land of Biarmia (the basin of the northern Dvina) first appears as a happy hunting-ground of Scandinavian pirates; later it is one of the principal tribute-paying dependencies of the city state of Novgorod. Similarly the drawing of the remoter areas into the trading network at first encouraged the formation of pirate and bandit gangs to prey on the caravans and the collecting centres; then it paid better for one or an alliance of such gangs to put down the others and establish "law and order" by exaction of tribute from the producers and tolls from the merchants: thus the pirates and bandits become military governments themselves engaged in trade, and learning to war with one another to obtain the proceeds of tribute, tolls and trade until the producers and merchants banded together with some other pirate or bandit force to make a new and more orderly government. At such times of crisis, long-ripening economic changes may come to fruition by political liberation from restraining powers: but this is of course a very different matter from supposing that this commerce and politics had any formative effect on the local economies.

At various times the merchants of both the non-slave economies of the peninsular lands and the slave economies on the continental route called in foreign military peoples to provide stable governments. Thus, typically, both the slave and the non-slave areas comprised (1) the agricultural producers living in stockaded or fortified hamlets and villages; (2) the craftsmen and local dealers living in garrisoned cities; and (3) the military government linking the garrisons, policing the trade-routes and collecting tribute in slaves and luxury goods from the forests and herds, with a permanent base in the local capital city but the government itself often on the move.

The building up of the peninsular trade route reached a new stage with the pioneering of the Dnieper and Volga river-routes; and once these were established as through routes with regular portages between the rivers, the problem of unification and policing became acute. Great-Russian legendary history tells of the driving out of Scandinavian pirates and the natural failure to form a single overriding state authority from among the competing trading cities, so that a joint embassy from a number of peoples around Novgorod—two Slav and three Finnish tribes—invited in the Scandinavian Rurik and his two brothers to form a military government, garrison the cities, police the rivers, and collect tribute. Norse legends in the sagas tell how pirate leaders accustomed to raiding in Biarmia were met and defeated by the wizard King of Novgorod. But the alliance of the local peoples with the merchants was naturally short-lived: when the new Viking government was installed, it took over the rule of Kiev and other cities on the river-routes as well as Novgorod, and it and the merchants were both interested in exactions. The old chronicler tells in his own way what this meant when he says that the

people of Novgorod were formerly Slavs (like the people
outside the city), but have become Vikings. This Viking
completion of the organizing of the river-routes was also the
completion of the making of the peninsular trade-circuit,
and East-Slav tradition rightly regarded it as the end of pre-
history and the beginning of history, nearly five generations
(as time was then reckoned) before the Slavs of Russia became
part of Christendom in A.D. 988.

History repeats itself in the slave lands of the continental
trade-circuit. Arab, Persian and Turkic military governments
garrison the cities and police sections of the route, fall out
over the profits and war with one another to the distress of
both producers and merchants. The final political unification
under a military government came in the thirteenth century,
when the two great trade-circuits were most closely interlinked
and the Fourth Crusade had captured Byzantium on behalf of
the Italian trading cities. The Turkic merchants of the Uigurs
in Central Asia brought in the Mongol military government of
Genghiz Khan and his sons, which drew together all the lands
from China to the Caucasus in the years 1211–26, and added the
western river-system in the years 1236–41. Thus Russia was
first united by the alliance of the continental merchants with
Mongol cavalry, Chinese military engineering, and the Turkic,
Caucasian and Slav administrative classes, under the name of
Tartary.

The two stages of the Mongol unification are markedly
different. The first under Genghiz Khan himself was cruel
and ruthless enough, but employed an effective political
intelligence system and an economical use of destruction.
The second stage, under Genghiz's grandson Batu in 1236–41,
is marked by neither of these characteristics: the Volga towns
and Kiev were sacked but—after some hesitation—not Novgorod (though this city was so alarmed at the fall of the Volga
towns that her merchants did not take up the herring awaiting
them at Yarmouth in 1238, thus causing considerable losses to
that city). This selective destruction of the trading and craft
centres on the river-system looks as though it is due to faulty
intelligence; but much worse was the fact that the conquerors
failed to protect their victims, and the conquered Slavs had to

defend themselves against the Swedes (whom they beat on the Neva in 1240), and the Teutonic Knights whom they beat on Lake Peipus in 1242. These stabs in the back are still a bitter historical memory for the Great-Russians, and their warrior prince Alexander Nevsky, who won these victories, is a great hero. The Teutonic Knights were a military-religious order recruited from all Western Christendom; Chaucer's "gentle parfit Knight" was one of them, for "oft had he raysed in Lettice and in Pruce"—raided in Lithuania and (Slav) Prussia.

The Mongol annexation of the river-system brought the fact of the existence of the new empire home to the politicians and traders of the west, and encouraged the aspiration for unification of the known world. The Pope conceived the possibility of converting the Mongols and with their aid wiping out both the infidel Saracens and schismatic or heretic Christians: his first embassy reached Karakorum in 1246. From that time onwards friendly relations were maintained between the Holy See and the Mongol capital at Karakorum, and later at Peking, and Franciscan missionaries visited many parts of the Far East. Bishop Nicholas of Peking in the fourteenth century had been a professor at Paris: he was a friar of the same order, and a member of the same university, as our own Duns Scotus.

This reaching out to a world unity appears more practically on the Mongol side, in the imposition of a unified administration over the whole vast area. But this administration was for purposes of extracting part of the product, not for developing production: taxation and conscription were universally imposed. Great wealth and power were thus concentrated in the capital and subcapital cities, but the concentrations were unproductive except for the small proportion of them which was expended in policing the trade-routes.

The three unseen weaknesses of united Tartary were its merely *political* unification of slave and non-slave economies without any development of a common *economic* organization; the competition of land with sea-borne traffic on the continental circuit; and the weakness of the Volga and Black Sea links between the continental and peninsular circuits. By the later years of the fourteenth century these weaknesses had in part become visible, and Tamurlane set out to reconstitute the organization: he very thoroughly destroyed the links between the circuits, redirecting the flow of trade from Samarkand to Syria, and concerned himself with India and China. By his time the vision of one unified world had receded, and he was a supporter of Islam against other views of the one world: for both practical and religious reasons he devastated Christian Georgia with extraordinary persistence, in 1393, in 1400, and again in 1403. In 1400 he had special maps of Georgia made, and so brought the great world into the highland villages of some of the homekeeping bandit tribes, including the Khevsurs, who have in our times retorted on the great world by sending out their most famous son, Stalin.

After Tamurlane had thus abruptly revealed the lack of organizational unity, old Tartary broke up into a number of states and peoples during the fifteenth century. The process of unification began again in the sixteenth; this time the lead came from the western side, and by the extension of western agriculture in the early stages provided the first pre-requisite for the permanent unification.

The East-Slav economy (of the Great, White and Little Russias) at the time it fell under Mongol rule may perhaps best be described as an allodial[1] natural economy traversed by important trade-routes and already containing within itself strong tendencies to feudalization. In the countryside the accumulation of allodial holdings into noble estates on which the former peasant allod holders were reduced to tenancy was already advanced; and almost all the remainder of the peasant allodial farmers were already "tribute"-paying subjects of the trading cities. That is to say, in the East-Slav area the development of closely knit economic relations between people was already well on the way to producing an equally closely knit political development as a counterpart to the economic, so that the political organization would no longer be just superimposed on the economies but would grow out of them and in

[1]Allodial land is held in absolute possession by right of clearance or inheritance and carries no rent or burdens of any kind. This tenure is pre-feudal.

turn assist their growth. The prospect of economic development in the East-Slav area was therefore very great: and the
economic forces did in fact make their way through in time
and grew their own political skin, so to speak, in spite of the
temporary and permanent devastations in the southern part
of the East-Slav river-system under Mongol rule.

During the first generation after the conquest, the Mongol
administration carried out a number of censuses which divided
the people into "tens", "hundreds", "thousands" and "ten
thousands": each unit provided the number of conscripts
given in its name, and paid taxes assessed on these same
numbers. These taxes were farmed out to Moslem merchants
from Central Asia, whose exactions in both Slav and Georgian
towns caused uprisings. The tax-farmers accordingly were
replaced by a Mongol bureaucracy, which operated for a
generation: then in the early fourteenth century, tax collection
was handed over to the native Slav authorities, under supervision by Mongol Residents. The innumerable royal dukes
of the house of Rurik had continued to exist in the early part
of the period, but they had very little to do (like the rest of the
previous ruling class): they occupied themselves with accumu-
lating allodial estates, developing self-sufficient and internally
diversified economies on them, and using the proceeds to
struggle against one another and bribe the Mongols. Meantime
trade, though not immediately handicrafts, began to revive:
the route from Novgorod to Sarai on the Volga ran through
Great-Russia, that from Riga to Surozh on the Black Sea
ran through Lithuania and White-Russia: both routes linked
up with the Hansa merchant cities. It was from the pure
Novgorod silver brought to London by these "Easterling"
merchants that our first sterling was named.

On the basis of this revived trade and further development
of rural production, the Great-Russian advance to feudalization
was resumed. In the fourteenth century the noble allodial
estates come to be subject to confiscation for treason both in
Novgorod and East Great-Russia; and the concept of subinfeudation (of vassals having vassals of their own) begins to
be formed in relations between the royal dukes, although still
expressed in the kinship terms of the allodial tradition: in 1375

and 1382 the Grand Dukes of Tver and Riazan declare themselves "younger brothers" to Moscow. This slight advance
however was again interrupted by Tamurlane's career, and its
effects: in the fifteenth century the disintegration of Tartary produced a network of Succession States of peoples and fragments
of peoples of very diverse origins and residence. The Cossack
communities of the Ukraine began at this time; devastated
Georgia split into three "kingdoms"; the Khanates of Kazan,
Crimea and Astrakhan, and the Hordes of the Uzbeks and
Kazakhs were established. The local trade from Novgorod
through Moscow to these various small communities remained
sufficient for Moscow to stand, in general, for the merchant
and the feudalizing interests as opposed to her rival Tver, a
stronghold of the noble allodial party. Consequently, the
formation of a feudal Great-Russia comes under the Moscow
dynasty.

It took twenty-five years of civil war (the Tartars and
Lithuania intervening) to establish the principle of organizing
the dynasty by primogeniture, so that the kingdom passes not
in equal divisions to all the sons but entire to the eldest son.
Vasily II finally won his point with the aid of two Tartar
princes whose prospects among their own folk were by now too
limited: they had first joined a Cossack community, then taken
service in Moscow. They were rewarded by the creation of the
vassal Khanate of Kasimov in 1452: Vasily was then a vassal of
the Khan of Sarai and at the same time the lord of that Khan's
brother in Kasimov.

As the feudalizing process advanced in east Great-Russia,
however, the trade of the Novgorod-Volga route was declining
with the fragmentation of Tartary, and the independence of
Novgorod also declined. Her ancient constitution no longer
provided the means of tackling problems: the popular assembly
had become a mob, the Soviet of Notables had ex-officio
seats for city officials and noble allodial representatives, but
none for the new feudal order. In 1478 Ivan III of Moscow
became suzerain of Novgorod: the popular assembly and the
Soviet ceased to function, and during the following years
the noble allodial estates outside the city were confiscated.
Their owners were settled on service fiefs elsewhere as feudal

tenants of the king, while the Novgorod noble allodial land was feu'd to new service tenants. (In 1510 the old free city of Pskov similarly came into feudal Muscovy.) These service fiefs were granted for occupancy only, and were not capable of subinfeudation—that is, the occupant could not take vassals of his own. Their occupants collectively formed the royal Household (*dvoryane*) and kept this name throughout the time (until 1861 and after) that they formed the ruling class of Russia. *Dvoryane* is the Russian word which is usually translated as "nobility" or "gentry". The Household does in fact resemble Western nobilities in that it is the landed and ruling class. Its cohesion, however, as the Household of the Tsar, distinguishes it from Western feudal nobilities and enabled it to hold down the slaves in the post-feudal period.

By the late fifteenth century the formation of feudal Muscovy was almost complete, and the experience of feudalization was general enough for questions of principle to emerge. These came up without any known communication between Russian thinkers and western feudal theory: mediaeval Russia was without knowledge of Roman law or Norman lawyers. Moreover, since the stabs in the back at the beginning of the Mongol period, everything Roman Catholic was heretical in Great-Russian eyes: the union of the Roman and Byzantine churches at the Council of Florence was regarded as Byzantine apostasy in Great-Russia, and from 1448 the Russian church regarded itself as independent of Byzantium and the last isolated defender of the only true faith: the Turkish capture of Byzantium in 1453 was proof to the Great-Russians that punishment visited apostasy. This view was reinforced by Great-Russia's success in liberating herself from the Tartar yoke in 1480, and the beginning of the return of the White-Russians to unity with Great-Russia, as in the drawing in of Pskov. The principles of feudalism thus began to be discussed in a fairly complicated situation: a reunited state of the three Russias was in prospect; the Russian church was the last stronghold of truth, and the extension of truth depended on the extension of the state, and this depended on the feudal development; at the same time national freedom and independence could not help but be inextricably linked in people's minds with allodial freedom as contrasted with feudal service; and finally, the Mongol exemption of monastery lands from taxation had meant that the church estates were the wealthiest and productively most advanced of all the lands: it was on these lands that the adscription (tying) of peasants to the soil began in the middle of the fifteenth century. In this respect therefore the church was the spearhead of feudalization, and it was on this point that the first discussion of feudal principles arose: whether the church should or should not own lands and serfs. The feudalizing party won a political victory in 1525, when the new Metropolitan of Moscow allowed Vasily III to divorce his childless wife in order to preserve the dynasty: the opposing party, the Non-Possessors (of land and serfs) were then denounced as heretics and traitors both, and extinguished by persecution. The alliance of the church, the dynasty and the Household completed the feudalization of Muscovy: in 1544 Ivan IV was proclaimed Tsar (Emperor) and in 1551, at the Council of Moscow, the church proclaimed that all other Christians were in error.

In 1552 the crusade for the reunification of Tartary under Moscow began with the conquest of Kazan, and the whole Volga route was subjugated in 1556. By 1579 the Cossacks were in Siberia and the north Caucasus; in 1589 the Metropolitan of Moscow became Patriarch of all the Russias. The peasant opinion of feudalism and of the national glories accruing is however made plain by the fact that in the Novgorod and central areas between a half and four-fifths of the villages that were inhabited before 1550 were deserted by the end of the century. This mass emigration of the peasants from noble allodial and feu estates alike enabled Ivan the Terrible to destroy the political resistance of the surviving allodial nobility (the Boyars); and then in 1581 to begin the nation-wide stage of adscripting the peasants. In 1597 the law was made more definite by permitting runaway peasants to be pursued and brought back at any time up to five years after their flight.

This agrarian revolution of the second half of the sixteenth century, carried through so blindly, found its immediate result in the famine and pestilence of 1601–3, and in the revolts, civil wars and wars with Poland that followed. The

situation of disorder was prolonged, but the victory of
feudalism was inevitable; the alliance of the church and the
Household finally won the day, and their triumph was codified
in the laws of 1649, when all estates became service fiefs and
all peasants were adscripted to the soil for life: all the land now
belonged to the Church or the Crown absolutely and to the
Household in fiefs. On this basis, Great-Russia prepared to
move forward again: the new Patriarch Nikon began in 1652
an attempt to turn the church national into the church imperial;
and in 1654 Little-Russia (the Ukraine) was formally united to
Muscovy. So in law the three Russian peoples were once more
under one rule, and their Crown already possessed considerable
lands in the Volga basin as well. The reality behind this was that
a single mode of agricultural production, based on Great-
Russia and rapidly extending southwards and eastwards, had by
now come into being: and from this time onwards the peasant
allodial colonizations continued to press beyond the frontiers,
then the frontiers would be extended to cover the newly
colonized areas and the marginal peoples; then more peasants
would seek allodial holdings beyond the new frontiers, and so
forth. So the nomad and slave economies were continually
pressed on by the Great-Russian peasant advance and depressed
by the advent of state power behind it: they had within themselves no forces capable of withstanding the establishment
of non-slave agriculture around and among them, and they were
increasingly impoverished. So nowadays the lands peopled by
the Great-Russians occupy all the east of European Russia from
the Baltic and the White Sea to the Caucasus and the Caspian,
then stretch in a long broad ribbon all through the wheatlands
of Siberia (south of the forest and north of the Asiatic steppe)
to Lake Baikal, and all down the Amur Valley, along the coast
of the Sea of Japan, and across the sea in southern Sakhalin and
southern Kamchatka. These wheatlands, and the railway system
that now links them, were established in the course of rather
more than three centuries, and re-unified the old Tartary
by establishing a common productive basis as the spine of the
area, in place of the former unification by trade-routes and
military government.

At the time when the mass emigration of the peasants from

the noble allodial estates was becoming established as a movement, in the winter of 1564–65, Ivan the Terrible joined in the movement by leaving Moscow, announcing that he gave up his kingdom and would let divine Providence choose his future abode. He explained that this decision was due to his distress at the treacheries, corruptions and robberies of the allodial nobility and of their abettors the clergy. This demonstrative departure and the manifestos explaining it both shared and voiced the activities and opinions of the migrating peasants; and both the immediate and long-term effects were immense. Immediately, the people asked Ivan to return, which he did but on condition that he had a free hand to deal with traitors (the allodial nobility), and that for this purpose there should be created a special Endowment of the Tsar's person with lands for the upkeep of the force he would raise to root out and execute traitors. In the blood-bath that followed, the local ties which bound the allodial nobility to their ancient estates were broken by confiscation, transportation and murder throughout the Endowment lands: Ivan was Terrible to the nobility and to the sinews of familiarity and tradition which held them to their allodial lands, but the fact that he had in some sense obtained a mandate for his terror, and that he was manifestly only one of the forces then destroying the noble allodial system, increased in importance through time. Ivan's dynasty came to an end with the death of his son and successor; but the struggle of the peasants against oppression thenceforward was always connected with names regarded as being those of Ivan's closest heirs, either his younger son Dmitry who died in childhood, or his in-laws the Romanov family, who did in fact finally provide the new dynasty founded by Michael the "Cossack Tsar" in 1613.

There grew up the firm conviction that Ivan's Endowment had been from the beginning intended to break the allodial nobility only in order that the old peasant allods should be restored; and each of the great peasant revolts embodied this belief in the person of some false Dmitry or Romanov; in times of no revolt (and particularly during the Emancipation) there was a constant conviction that the Romanov Tsar's policy was to restore the ancient allods to the peasants, but that this was frustrated by the Tsar's officials and the Household. This belief in the Crown was ended, finally, by the republican revolution of February 1917, and at that point the peasants repossessed themselves of the allods they had been waiting for so long. The elaborate and impressive title deeds of the collective farms, and the wording of their rights of tenure— use of the land in perpetuity and rent-free—must be understood in the light of this age-long struggle for the land by the Great-Russians, and to a lesser extent in the light of the fact that Islamic traditional law recognizes no private property in land, while the tribal nomad and hunting peoples were still at the primary allodial stage. This common ground between the various kinds of agricultural producers has a history going back to Ryazin's revolt in 1670–71, when Great-Russian peasants, Ukrainian and other cossacks, Turkic Christian Chuvashi and Turkic Moslem Bashkirs, Mongul Buddhist Kalmucks, Finnish heathen Mordvinians and Turkic Moslem Tartars all joined in common rebellion against feudal encroachments. Racialism has never been a natural vice in Russia, though pride of race and of cultural achievements is as universal, and local exclusiveness as marked, there as elsewhere; but these qualities, unlike racialism, do not at all exclude business-like co-operation whenever the work in hand requires it.

This absence of racialism was not, in the feudal and chattel slavery times, characteristic only of those who suffered a common oppression; it was equally characteristic of the body of common oppressors. Dynastic marriages between Great-Russian dukes and Tartar princesses prepared the way for the entry of Tartar princes and officials into Muscovite service as old Tartary was declining and Moscow was beginning to rise, and the shifting frontiers of Muscovy, Lithuania and Poland during the Mongol period and the reunification of the three Russias brought people of very different origins and pedigrees together in one ruling class. (For example, the White-Russian princely houses are all descended from our Princess Gytha, the daughter of King Harold who was killed at Hastings in 1066.) The period of feudalization transformed this class as a whole from an allodial nobility into the fief-holding Household: by the end of this process the Household contained the old noble houses (now fief-holding) and a considerable influx of new blood. At the same time, there developed a fantastically elaborate use of genealogies and pedigrees to determine the place of everybody in relation to everybody else in the Household, and all official appointments (except the higher military offices) were by custom bound to be made in accordance with a man's "place" in relation to his equals, superiors and inferiors. The intermarriages of new Household families with old added the complications of in-law computations to this "placing" system, and the actual inner structure of the Household by such precedences was intermittently further complicated by the constellations of blood and in-law relatives around the consorts of the dynasty. This fantastic method of appointments in the Household was only ended in 1682, and there is little doubt that the continuation of blood thus brought into prominence in the records has done much to obscure to later generations of scholars the nature of the process which transformed the allodial into the feudal nobility, and the feudal nobility into the slave-owning class. The same may be said of the use of the term Household both for the feudal nobility before 1675 and the slave-owning class thereafter. But in this latter case the continued use of the term maintained the fiction that the men of the Household were the creatures of the Tsar, holding office at his will, that will being the continued execution of the mandate given to Ivan the Terrible and renewed in the election of the Romanov "Cossack Tsar". The word which expressed this concept of the place of the Tsar in society was *samoderzhaviye*, which at first meant "self-determination" and independence of Mongol rule or of foreign intervention in general. Through Ivan the Terrible the word came to be applied to the Tsar's rule as guardian of the country against traitors, and Ivan elaborated his own theory of monarchy: he was God's earthly representative and his will represented God's will on earth; no constitutional and no ecclesiastical limits on that will could therefore be admitted in principle; this office had passed hereditarily from a brother of the founder of the Roman Empire to Rurik the founder of Viking rule and so to Ivan himself. This development of the theory was very well suited to the Household in later times when it wished to escape all the results of its irresponsibilities by holding itself out as being the mere creatures of the will of the monarch who was answerable only to God. It is because of this later development that *samoderzhaviye* is usually translated in English as "autocracy", but "self-existence" would be a nearer rendering.

The Russian church did not in the feudal period at all agree with Ivan's view of ecclesiastical subordination to the monarch. Just as Ivan claimed descent from Imperial Rome, so the church claimed that Russia was evangelized by St. Andrew, Peter's brother, and that all other churches had lapsed into heresy. The pretensions of the church and the dynasty were woven together in one theory, that Moscow was the Third (and final) Rome, and that the national congregation must keep its integrity by continuous observance of worship and prayer. In spite of Ivan's pronouncement, the church in a formal sense became responsible for the state at the beginning of the Romanov dynasty, when the new Tsar's father held the office of Patriarch of Russia (1619–33). This was merely formal in the sense that the elder Romanov had been forced into a monastery during the preceding troubles, and owed his high office entirely to political considerations; but in another sense the election of the Romanov father and son as Patriarch and Tsar was an expression of a very real and deep national feeling about the proper relations of the ecclesiastical and secular arms or aspects of the nation: both were expected to be expressions of the self-existence and integrity of the country.

By 1652 however the country was on the verge of further advances which would of necessity bring the Russian church into neighbourhood with other churches, and the newly chosen Patriarch Nikon endeavoured at one and the same time to make the ecclesiastical aspect of the nation superior to the secular, and to reform some details of the continuous observance and prayer. He might well have temporarily achieved his first objective, for the Tsar loved him and the Household were as willing to be under the wing of a Patriarch as under that of a Tsar; but his attack on the forms of ritual was taken as an attack on the national integrity and self-existence. The dispute was ferocious; it was formally settled in favour of Nikon's view, and the "Old Believers" were expelled from the church and persecuted. But in fact the real immediate victory lay with the Old Believers, who were the first Russian heretics that were not extinguished; and the long-term effect was the eating away in people's minds of the older conception of the national church. Not many members of the church were prepared to suffer persecution; but perhaps most sympathized with the persecuted, and after fifty years during which the church acted as a department of state the situation was openly avowed when Peter the Great abolished the Patriarchate and placed the church under the permanent rule of a government committee in 1721.

Peter the Great (1696–1725) was the only Tsar of the seventeenth and eighteenth centuries who was more master than servant of the Household. After his death however the Household gradually extended its powers, taking over everything that Peter had introduced. This meant that they ruled a Russia much stronger than before, and they had no difficulty in ending the church as an economic force in 1764, when its estates were secularized and it was deprived of the right to own peasants. This was almost a minor consequence of the great victory of the Household in 1762, when all legal obligations to give feudal service in return for fief estates were abolished: it was on these terms that Catherine the Great was placed on the throne. The theoretically absolute power of the monarch was from that date merely a cover for the actual absolute freedom and arbitrariness of rule exercised by the Household. Within both this theory and the actuality, the Crown became head of a professional executive without constitutional links with either the Household or any other element in the population so that in effect the three chief parts of the society (the Crown's executive, the Household and the commoners) were all in a constitutional sense isolated from one another: their only link was the individual person of the monarch, who was as an individual human being the only element in the country which had links with the several parts of society. This remained the principle of Russian political practice until 1917; its influence was apparent until 1953, and still is.

Napoleon's defeat in Russia and the entry of Russia into the councils of the world powers came at the time when the forces of the market were first becoming capable of making an impact on the organization of the country by the Household: one result was the rebirth of a national feeling and an attempt to state what Russia stood for in distinction rather than in hostility to other civilized lands. This attempt provided a three-word summary: *samoderzhaviye, narodnost, pravoslaviye* (usually translated as autocracy, nationality, orthodoxy). These words express respectively the qualities believed to be characteristic of the Tsar, the country as a whole, and the mind of the Great-Russian nation. Since they distinguished Russia from the West, these words harked back to the time before Peter's westernizing campaign, and referred to the nature of Russia as a community in being, of the people who composed it, and the mind that was right for them. Such large abstractions have the virtue of meaning all things to all men; they also ensured that discussion in nineteenth-century Russia should not be on any smaller questions. *Narodnost* thus might mean a conservative or fanatical nationalism, or a fellowship with the common people (the *narod*) which could begin to break down the slave-owning mentality inherited from the eighteenth century—a use for example of the Russian (instead of the French or German) language by educated people, the making of Russian as distinct from the performance of Italian music, and so forth. It is because the classics of Russian literature have *narodnost* in this sense, and because none of them are even as far back in the past as Burns is in Scotland, that they are still a living literature to the Russians much more than Shakespeare is in England: their matter is not yet fully digested and absorbed into the thought of the nation. Dostoievsky's work, for example, looked deep into Russian life and in a sense far back into Russian history, and modern Russia is as yet far from having come to terms with the memories and realities which Dostoievsky presents.

There are very many things in modern Russia which strike the outside observer as—to say the least—being nothing like what he expected of a country claiming to be socialist,

G

or at any rate claiming to provide a better way of life than is found outside. These claims have aroused derision and mistrust for three separate sets of reasons. One of these sets may be summed up as practical ignorance: there is not much knowledge abroad in this country of what sort of people the Russians are, and what has gone to their making; and there is probably less knowledge abroad in Russia of the sort of people we are, and what has gone to our making. The second set of reasons may be called theoretical in the widest sense within the working-class movement of the two countries: we believe we know the qualities a working class should have and those that socialism will have. The Russians believe equally fundamentally in their own knowledge in these matters. The two bodies of knowledge however do not coincide, and the noise of the grinding of axes is loud in both lands. It is long overdue in both places that we should each consider what sort of people the other is, and what has gone to the other's making.

There is no allodial peasant tradition here: but the peasant revolution in 1917 was one of the most important elements in the total upheaval. We have no background of slavery in our industrial tradition, and we industrialized long ago, and our capitalism is old, experienced and wary; we have no recent experience of the savage ex-peasant capitalist bully, and no newly lighted passion for the achievement of skills. We have a thousand years of continuous development of religious, legal and political thought, disputation and skill, and a century of general literacy: it is difficult to remember that the most fortunate of the Russian peoples has little more than a century of continuous development in these matters, and less than a lifetime of widespread literacy. We have in Great Britain three peoples, all with a long common history, one common language, and a common economy; in Russia there are some hundred and fifty peoples with diverse histories, different languages, and, before the "construction of socialism", different economies. It is in fact fairly obvious that with the most determined good intentions in the world, the ideas about what a working class is, and what socialism is, are likely to be rather different in Russia and this country, and that neither will be quite wrong according to its own lights.

The third set of reasons lies in politics outside working-class and socialist movements and—apart from high politics—mostly in the "middle-class" groups in the two countries. These reasons are a mixture of socialist theory and general cultural activity in both countries, and both middle classes tend to be rather superior about each other if given half a chance: there is a natural professional rivalry, embittered to a certain extent by the proletarian origins and affiliations of the Russian middle classes, who are far from having all the expertize and mastery that our own professionals have, but who show sometimes a sign of something beside which expertize and mastery are merely a question of time and detail.

These three sets of reasons taken together are not however the whole of the problem of understanding what sort of people the Russians are and what has gone to their making. The general overriding element in the problem, to which particular things come down time after time, is a widespread, diffuse, but quite certain knowledge in this country that the Russians lack something without which we do not hold a country can be a country at all. If we give this a name, we most often call it democracy, or tolerance, or live and let live: it is a practical knowledge of the comfortable and uncomfortable ways in which the various parts of society rub up against each other and go on living together, often in mutual disapproval. In Russia, mutual disapproval if it is strong enough means that different groups do not go on living together: one or the other is condemned to death.

The story of how Christianity came to Russia ten centuries ago has two parts: the first tells of the political conversion of the prince of Kiev and his people, and of the destruction of the heathen idols. The second part tells of what happened when he died: his eldest son was a heathen, and of doubtful legitimacy, and set out to secure his succession by the ancient method of killing as many of his half-brothers as he could reach. One of these, Boris, was an excellent young prince, and was told of his danger; his own warriors wanted him to fight for his life and the crown. But he held that for a Christian faced with the choice between fratricide and death there was no question which he should do; and, deserted by his warriors, he was put to the sword by one of his brother's henchmen. A few days later, the same choice was put to another brother, Gleb, and he made the same decision. Their fate soon became known throughout the Russian land, and the Greek bishops and learned clerics who were running the Russian church were faced with an imperious popular demand that the two saintly brothers should be canonized. Five years after their death, the Metropolitan of Kiev gave way; but fifty years later another Greek Metropolitan was still doubtful whether right had been done, for Boris and Gleb were candidates for canonization not because they were martyrs, or ascetics, or theologians: they were "passion bearers" and the infant Russian Christianity had produced this new kind of saint without permission from the experienced mother church. The church in Russia plainly has had most rich opportunities: its whole history shows they have never been properly taken—but a people who could make these saints ten centuries ago will not have lost its vision meantime. If this vision has found no outlet in the church, we must try to recognize the way it has found elsewhere.

The choice between a sin of commission and death in the body was a hard but not a difficult choice for Boris and Gleb: the choice is a matter on which the subtlest doctors of the western churches have not agreed when the decision has to be made between a sin of omission in some responsibility for others, and the danger of death of the soul. The Russian church had no such guidance to offer its members; yet there has not been a generation in Russian history when such decisions had not to be made by the rulers of the country; and of most of them it would be said (by such historians as would be prepared to consider the question) that if men who committed their crimes were not in peril of their souls, that phrase has no meaning at all. But the Russians, rulers and ruled alike, have in their own ways understood the problem very well; and there has been a silent but completely known understanding of a moral division of labour between the rulers who imperil their souls as an occupational hazard, and the ruled who are the simpler passion-bearers. This relationship of the parts of society is not democracy or tolerance or live and let live; but it is something of no lesser worth in human affairs, and it is

still the living faith of Russia. When Stalin spoke of the first
five-year plan as the passion of the country, he was not talking
in highly coloured language, but remembering and recalling
that the workers and peasants were the countrymen of Boris
and Gleb. When the Public Prosecutor's office in December
1953 spoke of the hounding and harrying of innocent people
by the political police under Beria, and the persecution of
Ordjonikidze's family, there was not only the silent promise
that this sort of thing was being ended, but also the certain
knowledge that the making of socialism also takes its quota of
passion-bearers.

The first thing that has to be understood about Russian
Marxism is that, whereas the church in Russia failed to
provide the thought and learning which the Russian people's
knowledge required, Russian Marxism is providing such thought
and learning, and at the same time also the thought and
learning that is needed for simpler sciences than ethics, those
of nature, of technology, of economics and politics.

We have seen how during the nineteenth century the
slave-owning mentality began to be broken down among some of
the educated people (the lower-ranking and more decent members of the now very large Household and young people of
families "outside the ranks" of the Household), and how
nothing less than the fundamental principles of social and
national life were under discussion. The central problem was
how and by what means Russia could move forward from the
old-fashioned and outmoded *samoderzhaviye, narodnost, pravoslaviye*, without throwing away everything that had gone to her
making: in short, how she could develop while keeping her
identity, and in that sense how she could become different
while remaining herself. Exactly the same problem of course
faced all the other communities which were becoming capitalist
at that time: and that group of countries including Russia
consequently saw the problem of becoming capitalist very
differently from how England had seen it a couple of centuries
earlier: for England, with her peculiar feudal tradition distin-
guishing her from the rest of Europe, to become more different
from her neighbours was to become more fully herself. For
France in the next century, with industry and trade as fully

developed before her political revolution as England's was at the same date more than a century after the English political revolution, the problem was not imitation of England, but the fighting out of the struggle for rulership between her feudal and capitalist classes. But for the latecomers to industry, with the immediate results of English industrialization before their eyes, the question was not so simple. In particular, these countries had very large peasant populations but England had wiped out her peasantry, a process against which German and Russian humanity revolted, and in that revulsion greatly strengthened their feudal nobilities against their rising capitalist classes. To become different and remain herself was first Germany's, then Russia's, overriding problem.

There are two levels on which such a problem can be attacked: the practical and piecemeal level, and the level of principle. At the second, the first question that needs to be settled is what is "difference" and what is "self-hood", that is, these concepts need to be rationally analysed. In the language of German philosophy of the time, the rational analysis of concepts was the "dialectics of ideas" and the fullest development of this line of thought was carried out by Hegel in the philosophy of dialectical idealism. One of Hegel's main arguments was that throughout the history of philosophy, every fresh idea that came forward was only part of the truth; consequently there soon followed the opposite idea, and these two fought together until it was seen that each was part of a single deeper truth which embraced them both. This, said Hegel, is the universal single law followed by ideas in their movement and history; and—he went on—if we apply this law to the concepts of "selfhood" and "difference", we see that every idea plainly is itself, has "self-hood", and by developing becomes not only "different", but produces its own opposite. The pair of opposite ideas is a Contradiction, and the fighting out of the Contradition produces in time the single deeper Ground of new development. Hegel went into many fields of ideas and showed that this law applied everywhere, as he thought. For the countries that were struggling to become different and at the same time remain themselves, Hegel's work was like a revelation, since it showed not only that they must in fact be doing both, but in thinking that they were doing either, they must be doing the other as well. Hegel's work opened up floodgates of effort in countries that had before been lost and confused; and generations of young students all aflame with the new ideas began hopefully to work out their countries' problems. They soon discovered that their beliefs were regarded with approval so long as they confined themselves to showing that the existing states of affairs were the outcome of long histories of successfully solved Contradictions; but that as soon as they pointed out that these Grounds were breeding new Contradictions (that ideas held in universal respect were only partly true and that the diametrically opposite ideas had some truth in them also), then they ran into trouble of all kinds, in their personal affairs, in getting teaching jobs, or in politics. Britain, where nobody had any idea what it was all about, became the chosen home of German and Russian political and philosophical refugees, and the Continent seethed with underground writings forbidden by the censorships of various countries.

These young men had been working on the assumption that as soon as people saw the truth, then they acted on it. When this touching faith in the power of pure reason was disabused, the question of course arose: where did Hegel go wrong? Quite a number of answers to this question were suggested, and the one that provoked most discussion was that when Hegel showed that the development of the idea of God had historically obeyed his universal law, he took the idea of God purely intellectually, as a concept to be analysed; whereas what he ought to have done was to show that the development of the idea of God had been part of the development of human ways and hopes of life. This argument of Feuerbach's united the French revolutionary rationalist tradition with the Hegelian philosophy of ideas, and was a second revelation to the eager young men of the more backward European countries. Needless to say, it made their notions even more obnoxious to the authorities.

The next step in bringing Hegel down to earth was made by Marx, who began with Feuerbach's point about human ways and hopes of life, and worked on the problem of applying Hegel's dialectical law of development to the human communities who are the possessors of ways and hopes of life.

To do this, he used another side of the French revolutionary tradition, the work of French thinkers on the political class divisions of society; and brought in also the work of British political economists on the interrelationships of groups of people both in production itself and in their ownership of the elements of the economy. In his analysis of economies and societies he had two main arguments: that the economy was the skeleton and the society the flesh of the community and that this pair of elements in the community was a pair of opposites each acting on the other but with the source of newness almost always in the economy; and that in the economy the classes owning and the classes not owning the means of production formed another pair of opposites always, even if unknowingly, struggling to resolve the Contradiction between them and by that struggle at one time imperceptibly and at another by a landslide changing the whole structure of the economy; and that when the skeletal framework changed the flesh also took on a new shape. Bringing this down to political practice, Marx argued that capitalism was evolved out of feudalism, and that in turn socialism would be evolved out of capitalism; within feudalism the merchant class developed and by its activities transformed the relations of the other classes to one another, then changed the nature of production and turned the peasantry into a proletariat; this new class in turn would change the capitalist economy into a socialist one.

The young people of the educated class in Russia, already familiar with the Hegelian dialectics of ideas, found no difficulty in understanding how Marx's analysis applied to western Europe, but debated hotly whether it held for Russia. They wrote and asked Marx whether Russia, just beginning her capitalist development, would have to go through all the miseries of the destruction of the peasantry which the British Isles had experienced. Marx replied that the answer depended on whether the existing village-community organization among the Russian peasantry with its communal ownership of land was strong enough to "regenerate Russia". In other words, Marx through this and other letters told his Russian correspondents to use his analytical method on the facts of Russian life, and not to take over lock, stock and barrel the results of his work on the West European economies. Since that time, Russian Marxism has embraced both those who took Marx's advice, and those who took his results: but even the second group took his results with Russian eyes. The struggle of classes meant, for example, the hunting down of allodial nobles by the Endowment men of Ivan the Terrible, or the revolts of peasants of several peoples led by Ryazin and Pugachov; capitalism meant the spidery finances of Witte, the projected destruction of the mass of the peasantry by Stolypin, the calculating lecheries and cunning of Rasputin, and the heavy fist of the railway contractor.

Marx's answer to his Russian questioners centred in effect on a question of political timing: whether the Russian working class could be brought up to scratch before peasant collective property dissolved under the impact of the market. Russian capitalist industry was a very small part of the total economy, and the working class that existed was, to most Russian eyes, no more than a special part of the peasantry, just as the old slave and serf outwork and mining villages were special parts of the slave and serf peasantry. The people who took Marx's advice thus had as their first job to decide whether the industrial labour-force was still part of the peasantry or already constituted a working class. This question involved also the degree of differentiation within the peasantry itself; and this analysis had, following Marx's advice, to be done at a time when none of the various groups being studied (capitalist, worker, peasant) had any established knowledge of themselves as interrelated groups. The question was consequently discussed at a highly theoretical level, and only *after* its settlement at that level did the disputants join forces with the workers: as a result the workers became widely conscious of their future alternatives almost before they had become conscious of their own existence as a class.

From this situation there came a number of developments due to specific Russian conditions. In the first place, the conscious socialist movement consisted of intellectuals who were, to their own government, unconscionable trouble-makers, and who were, consequently, always being exiled to various country parts, on the margins of the central areas or in Siberia.

But the growth of the railways meant that in most of the central areas and in parts of Siberia and Central Asia there was a scattering of railway and other industrial workers, among whom revolutionary exiles or emissaries could find useful political work to do. Consequently, socialist theory tended to spread with the working class into every industrial cranny of the economy, but to retain a highly conscious appearance without very deep roots in the natural self-awareness of the workers: the natural workers' movement indeed remained very near to the peasant level. The so-called trade union movement of these early years, for example, was in the main a transplantation to the factory of village organization; and the meeting and mutual influence upon one another of this natural organizational mode and high theory produced four consequences which have given much of her shape to modern Russia.

The first of these is that by far the greatest contribution to the nature of modern Russia has come from one of her peoples only, the Great-Russians of the wheatlands and railway lines where capitalist trade and industry and the working class were first rooted, and from the Great-Russian labour force of such outlying main areas of capitalist industry as the oil fields of the Caucasus and the cotton ginning of Central Asia. The Great-Russian contribution has to a considerable extent been masked to foreign observers by the eminence of non-Great-Russian intellectuals on the theoretical side of the movement; and by the fact that, given the actual size of the Great-Russian contribution, the principle of equality of peoples within modern Russia has been double-edged: it means not only that the Great-Russians were not to exploit less advanced peoples, but also that an obligation lies on less advanced peoples to move far more quickly than is comfortable to parity of skill and organization with the Great-Russians.

The second result of the nature of the workers' own movement and awareness was the emergence in 1905 and 1917 of the "soviet" form of public authority. "Soviet" is an old Russian word meaning to take "counsel together"; the name was given as we have seen to the Soviet of Notables in the old free city of Novgorod; and it was often used for special committees of the Household in Tsarist times. It is a "committee" in our sense of the word in that authority is committed to it, but it carries the connotation of appointment rather than election in the sense that members even of an elective soviet are chosen for the forces and groups they represent, the offices they hold, or the weight they carry in some particular field of work: the hustings element is lacking in the Russian tradition as embodied by this word. (Insofar as a hustings tradition had taken root or was aspired to in Russia, it was manifested in the restricted elections to and debates of the Duma after 1905: this name means a "meditative body".) As a working-class organization a soviet retains the idea of a committee of solid people, of the larger personalities, stronger characters, or more experienced members of the elective body; and the nowadays elaborate and varied processes of pre-election selection of candidates for nomination do to some extent accord with this tradition. To the ordinary Russian voter, the pre-election machinery gives the election itself the solemnity and weight of a ceremonious and formal ratification— with, of course, the danger of the selection process being at fault. If the selection process develops too many faults (either within itself or because it is not keeping up with the people) the Russian voters may in the future insist that the election itself should do the weeding out between candidates, and if this happens it may look as though they were adopting elections of the western type. But we should, in that case, not be deceived by mere appearances: the voters will still expect the elected body to be of the traditional "soviet" type, consisting of the solid people of the local or national community.

The third result of the nature of the workers' own movement and awareness is the conception of the factory as a community, like the village. This conception takes institutional form in the trade union branch, whose nature and work we have discussed in Chapter IV; and the community centres in Russian towns are the factory clubs.

The fourth result of the nature of the workers' own movement and awareness appeared first in a problem. The transplantation of village organization into the factories meant in the early days that the factory organizations were very unstable: people came into and went out of the embryo trade unions as they came into and went out of jobs; and these illegal trade unions, and the workers' more spontaneous factory and inter-factory committees, came into and went out of existence accord-ing to the rise and fall of distress, prosperity and political excitement. The people on the theoretical side of the move-ment were no less unstable, though for the different reason that theory is as likely to produce bees in the bonnet and per-sonal quarrels as it is likely to produce unity of aim and subordination of personal affairs. The problems of getting a working-class political party organized and keeping it in being were therefore very great indeed. This was why the principle of "democratic centralism" was put forward, which has aroused so much criticism outside Russia: its purpose was to prevent people floating in and out of the party, to secure orderliness in delegations and elections, to stop empire-building inside the party and to prevent groups that broke away in fact from still sheltering under the party's name and authority. During the first generation of the party (1903–29) it had in practice almost nothing to do with opinions: in our terms, Lenin's party in-cluded people from Liberals to Anarchists; and it became "monolithic" with the emergence of a new working class out of industrialization, and with the rooting of theory in the ex-perience and self-awareness of this new working class.

In brief, the Marxism which went into Russia by way of the eager young people in the nineteenth century has been put through the mill of Russian working class and peasant experience and self-awareness in the twentieth: and the problem of how Marxism can become different and retain its selfhood is nowadays the problem of working classes outside Russia.

The mill through which the Russians have put Marxism has ground exceedingly quickly and not always very fine. Marx himself in 1881 recommended his correspondents to work for the development of peasant collective ownership, but the pressure of Russian peasant aspirations forced the Socialist Revolutionaries to base their programme on equaliza-tion of private property in land; in 1917–18 the peasants achieved this by their own actions, and the Bolsheviks had to agree. This final triumph of the allodial tradition (as modified by many centuries of non-allodial society) was feared by the Bolsheviks as providing a teeming soil for the natural re-growth of capitalism in the countryside and we have seen in Chapter III that this view either exaggerated or radically misunderstood the nature of peasant aspirations. It would further appear that since the peasants themselves forced the socialist politicians to abandon Marx's recommendations in politics, the Marxist historians have clung with all the more tenacity to Marx's results in his observations in various places on the economic history of Russia: they have the excuse that Marx was remarkably well-informed on this subject for a nineteenth-century west European. But of course much more material is available now, and is continually increasing with the publication of primary sources and archaeological work; while comparative anthropology is a science which was only being born in Marx's time. This flow of knowledge is visibly bursting the seams of Marx's historical results for Russia in, for example, Lyashchenko's *History of the Russian National Economy*, and it may be expected that the traditional Marxism of this field of work will soon be put through the mill, just as Marx's policy recommendations on contemporary Russia were.

The traditional Russian pattern of statecraft, as developed in her feudal and slave-owning periods and degenerating in her full capitalist period, was in the early days of Russian Marxism to a considerable extent well encompassed by a single-minded interpretation of the Marxist theory of the state as a resultant of economic forces and as the executive of the dominant economic class. The collapse and forcible destruction of the Tsarist state machinery of rule were very thorough, but the civil service personnel were retained in large numbers, because in a largely illiterate country they were capable of the necessary clerical work. Marxist theory, as is well known, looked forward to the "withering away of the state" during the development of socialism, i.e. with the approach to a classless society; and this forecast became entangled with a good many political debates in the twenties and thirties. Since however all the serious politicians of whatever persuasion were naturally keenly aware of governmental responsibility once the period of war communism was over, the main noise came from the

theorists among the lawyers. (It is to be remembered that
in Russia, as in many other East European countries during
their capitalist periods, the fact that the lawyers are almost
the only highly literate people in the countryside tends to
make a large proportion of them politicians as well: several
"peasant parties" in those countries have consisted almost
entirely of lawyers.) These Russian lawyers believed themselves concerned professionally and immediately with the
withering away of the state: for if the state withered, so would
the law. This anarchistic doctrine continued to be preached
under the name of Marxism until the middle thirties, in glaring
contrast to the rapid development both of a complex administration and of the political police. In fact of course the debate
was not about Marxism at all, but used some words of Marx's
to express one side of the old allodial tradition which in earlier
times had been expressed in the emigration of peasants beyond
the state frontiers and in the doctrine of the Old Believers that
Peter the Great and his successors fulfilled the prophecy of the
reign of Antichrist.

Marx's concentration on economic analysis meant, for the
Russian users of his results rather than his method, that the
economic aspect of the functions of the state often took
the place in their minds of a more fully considered view of
the state as having social as well as economic aspects. Moreover, at the same time as the social aspects of the new Russia
were rapidly coming into being and developing, the number of
nations and peoples within the new society was becoming
something to be emphasized: so the word "nation" could not be
used for the whole society; while Marx's comment that the
working men have no country (in a certain sense true, but only
of the most embitteredly intelligent of recently expropriated
peasants) made it impossible for the users of Marx's results to
employ the word "country" in the sense of "motherland". And
yet, with industrialization, the new working class was coming to
a lively appreciation of having and managing a country. On
this point therefore Marxism and Russia came to an uneasy
compromise: Russia is a country of many nations under a
single government, and this fact is represented by the words
"multinational state" (which, if it were purely Marxist,

would mean only that the government and civil service were staffed by people from many nations). The same contradictory phrase is also now used to describe the Tsarist empire. The confusion of thought reflected in this phraseology does not stop there: fashion among the historians, influential of recent years but now beginning to wane, treats the successive advances of the Tsarist frontiers not only as having had a fortunate outcome in the end (which would be a natural view for them to take), but also as having conferred benefits on the conquered at the time; so that the various national revolts against these unwelcome benefits are defined as "reactionary", and much effort is spent on studying the background of their leaders (who, if they were at all educated people, necessarily got their education from priests or mullahs as Stalin did, or came from a landowning family). This historical fashion is in part a reaction against an earlier view that the Tsarist conquests were an unmitigated evil for the conquered peoples, which may have been true in the short run, but of course cannot be upheld in the long run by any patriotic Russian today.

These are just the most obvious examples of the way in which Marx's results in his study of the state have been put through the mill of Russian experience. Plainly, the mill has still much work to do.

On the side of the practice and theory of statecraft itself, both the Marxist and the Russian traditional elements have been far more substantial. When Ivan the Terrible put forward his views on Divine will and his own will as its representative, he was using the usual mediaeval turn of thought in an attempt to make clear the fact that a country or a class is rarely a free agent, and that its responsible authorities are only too aware of this. Exactly the same turn of thought was far more fully elaborated in other mediaeval states, and through this work came into full consideration by Hegel and, more practically, by Marx. For Hegel, working in the realm of ideas, and believing that the development of ideas followed the universal dialectical law, human freedom of the reason could not lie in the *direction* taken by men's thoughts, but only in their certainty and scope in relation to thoughts that had gone before and would come after: the illusory freedom of direction was thus replaceable by a real freedom which arose out of knowledge of "necessity", the inescapable movement of ideas. For Marx, any single economic relationship of men was a moving part of the whole economic structure. This structure came into existence, developed, and passed away without intervention of human will as such deliberately and knowingly undertaking the construction of it and able to dispense with or choose its consequences. Given a certain general level of technology, productiveness demands a certain structure of economic relations, and knowledge of this fact gives men a freedom they had not previously possessed, namely, the freedom to direct their energies to the advance of skill, to bringing the shape of society into a fruitful relation to the shape of the economy, to pressing forward the study of these matters, or such other activity as can be *known* to be the next pre-requisite of human progress, and its success soberly foreseen. Thus Ivan's declarations and his securing of a mandate from the people, and their experience that the giving of the mandate led to their enserfment and soon to their enslaving, are fully taken up and satisfyingly explained both in themselves and as a pre-requisite to the people's taking of their fate into their own hands in 1917, when knowledge of the working of society transformed an otherwise unforeseeable chance into a seized opportunity for the exercise of a dedicated freedom of choice. And, for the Russians, this knowledgeable freedom continues in their constant pursuit of skill; and the weaker brethren for whom this pursuit is involuntary, or for whom it is merely the means of satisfying personal ends, are given few opportunities of avoiding enlightenment.

If the first revolution led by Marxists had been a simple working-class revolution in an industrialized country, the differences between using Marx's results and using his method would have taken a long time to become evident. The Russian upheaval, by contrast, was very complex, embracing at once four changes each of which, if it had occurred separately, would have been called a revolution. There was the peasant revolution which took the form of appropriating household allods; there was the working-class revolution which was political at the time and economic for the future industrialization; there was the revolution in ideas which set a sober method of inquiry over against all the various preconceived notions of how people ought to behave, whether these notions were religious or secular, Christian or Moslem or pagan, old and conservative or novel and enthusiastic; and there was also the revolution of the peoples against Tsarism and Great-Russification.

The revolution of the peoples took various forms according to their past history and their current economic stage. In White-Russia for example its outstanding characteristic was a local cultural nationalism expressed very largely in literary forms, political discussions and educational theories. In the Ukraine, where Great-Russification had a particularly bad history, there was a strong separatist movement. In the Caucasus nationalist and separatist governments were established, and overthrown. In Asia the fighting along the railway lines left the border peoples independent for a time, in the course of which the other claimants to rule re-asserted their authority: in fact the civil wars there had already begun with the Central Asian revolt in 1916 against the Tsarist call-up. As the fighting died down, the first necessity was to get production started again, and the central government (being well aware of the economic roots of the friction between the Great-Russian and other nationalities) put out much effort, for example, to attract local people into factory work (where this existed) until then manned almost entirely by Great-Russians. Much effort was also expended in the opening up of educational institutions in the main national centres: the epic tale of the founding of the University of Tashkent includes not only the getting together in Moscow of a staff, library and equipment, but a journey by train of these men and materials which lasted over a year through bandit-infested country, over broken bridges and ruined lines; then the starting of the teaching work with full-time students who were already literate, and the greater part of teaching devoted to extra-mural work among semi-literate and illiterate adults of the native Uzbek population. The first few Uzbeks who graduated from extra-mural to full-time study were the sign that the University had found its feet.

In the countryside the gradual spread of medical and school networks, the campaign against adult illiteracy, the devising of

H

alphabets for peoples who had no written language, the
starving of the central areas of printing machinery and printing
workers so that what was produced could go out to places
where there were none of either, all helped substantially to
change the old tradition of friction. But the widespread banditry
that was a legacy of the civil and interventionist wars retained
enough of a nationalist colouring in some areas for the gangs to
serve as rallying points against collectivization, especially in
nomad and semi-nomad areas. In these places, the ignorance
of the young townsmen in charge of collectivization had particularly catastrophic results: the nomad peoples were settled
so that they could not take their herds to the seasonal water-holes,
and the animal wealth of these areas was in part destroyed.
This was not however a totally unmixed evil: with the ending of
nomad life, large-scale banditry was also ended, and also some
of the more picturesque and lawless customs of these parts.
Law and order were often imposed by highly unorthodox means:
one local administrator proved his worth by ending the blood-
feud in his area, where it was not only an immemorial custom,
but was exacerbated by the fact of a mixed population of
Christians and Moslems. A number of successful feuders had
been sent to prison, but this was proving no deterrent, and
the local party secretary took the matter in hand. He did a
great deal of reading for a time, and then called a joint meeting of all the local priests and mullahs, to whom he said:
"I have now read all your holy books; and I find that nowhere
in them is the blood-feud laid down as a religious duty,
although both your peoples believe that it is. So, the next time
there is a feud killing, it is not the ignorant killer but his
teachers who will go to prison." The preaching of the several
scriptures was done with such thoroughness thereafter that
there were no more feud killings.

In more settled and sophisticated areas the task of elementary enlightenment was undertaken by an enthusiastic
but somewhat inept body called The League of the Battling
Godless, which set out to end the reign of superstition among
the more benighted. In spite of its terrifying name it was on the
whole a worthy body in its own way, providing simple lantern
slide lectures on evolution, the origin of the earth, and the errors

of witchcraft, for the villages and collective farms. I once visited their head office in Moscow in company with a wealthy Dutch rationalist of Jewish extraction, who reproached the officials there with the fact that the congregations at the two Moscow synagogues were large. "Ah, but," said the Battling Godless, "didn't you notice that the women are beginning to carry handbags even on the Sabbath?" It was a few months after this that the League was closed down by the government. From what I saw of its work, its attack on immemorial rustic superstitions is not distinguishable in practice from, say, that of the better parish priests in Ireland, though the philosophical presuppositions are of course quite different. In the overspill of revolutionary zeal amongst the intellectual politicians and their younger followers, especially in the resurgence of this zeal during collectivization, the League of Battling Godless organized children's demonstrations of mockery against the cherished religious beliefs of their parents, but the League did not remain an organization of serious importance after that phase of its activities. The anti-religious struggle became a more political affair in the collective farms, when local party leaders were blamed by headquarters in Moscow for failing to undermine the influence of the priests, who were able to get the farmers to observe all the innumerable Saints' days during the harvesting season (which they had never done when farming on their own account), for this could amount to a general agricultural strike in whole areas. The war brought great changes; religion is still argued against loudly and rudely enough, but the Army has its chaplains and the Patriarchate of the Orthodox Church has been restored for the first time since its abolition by Peter the Great. The old Great-Russian hatred of Catholicism, dating from the time of the stab in the back by those "gentle parfit knights" who "raysed in Lettice and in Pruce", is still as strong as ever, and the Uniat church in the recently annexed territories has been re-absorbed into the Orthodox: these are not religious questions for the Russians, but political and patriotic—the Uniats in their view are "rice Christians" now liberated from the need for pretence.

Modern Russia's own "gentle parfit knights" have been her political police. (The term "secret police" is a misnomer:

there can rarely have been a less secret organization. One of their officers was astonished that I, a foreigner, did not know that they always gave telephone numbers backward.) The political police were founded and organized by Dzerzhinsky to work on the basis of the internal passport system and the house committees. Every resident in Russia has his identity card, which he carries on his person and must produce on request by the police. He must get it stamped both out and in when- ever he moves from one police district to another, even on holiday or visiting. The house committees are elected by all adult members of families in a big house or block, and are responsible for what goes on under their roof—for example, people staying the night with relatives or friends should be reported to the house committee. This systematic enlistment of neighbourly curiosity into the security service by Dzerzhinsky supplemented the Tsarist system of *concierge* intelligence, and was regarded by the more politically minded among the workers as extremely democratic in that everybody was brought into the work of guarding the state. This feeling became strongest during the war, when it was expressed in the story of how a Moscow housewife caught a German woman spy because the Russian woman noticed in the other's string shopping bag a jar of honey of a brand made in her sister's village in the Ukraine that was in German hands. Another and more elaborate story with the same moral is the tale of the seven German spies in the Moscow underground. A woman and her friend standing in the queue for the train were watching a group of uniformed police, and giggling. A plain-clothes man came up to them and asked what was funny. "Well," said one of the women, "my husband is a policeman ,but his boots are not like those," and she pointed to the uniformed men. "No more they are," said the plain-clothes man, "but don't show you've noticed anything,'" and off he went to phone. The platform was surrounded and the suspected men arrested: and they were seven German spies, who had found they could not get lodgings anywhere (because of the house committee system) and had been living in the underground because it was warm there, and they could get food from the trolleys on the platforms.

Wartime working-class stories like this give, of course,

only part of the picture. There were the political police also in peacetime, and there are other people beside the working class. The weight of the great purge of 1936–38 fell on the "middle-class" intellectual groups mainly, and on the political police themselves. It is extremely difficult to get any clear idea of the number of people involved: in Moscow in 1936–37 we were always hearing of large numbers of arrests in Leningrad or some other town, for example that the entire staff of a college had been picked up in one night, but the most impressive stories were always at second or third hand—much like the stories we told in London during the war of the bomb that fell in the next street. An economics research institution with a staff of a hundred where I taught English and studied planning lost nobody except its formal head, who was mixed up in high politics, and myself, who as a foreigner could not stay on when the security mania reached its pitch at the end of 1937. But whatever the total numbers were, there is no doubt that many of the people involved were guilty, at the most, of folly, and in probably the majority of cases of merely being denounced by others under pressure of the political police or to wipe off old scores.

The nervous strain of the gradual accumulation of suspicion around a man produced an immediately recognizable half hang-dog, half defiant, look so that everyone could tell he was going to be picked up in a few days: and the falling away of friends, and those friends' own conflicts of fear and friendship, of public and personal loyalties, was a miserable business. The actual arrest in these cases often came as a relief to the victim and to his friends—until one and then another of the friends began to be taken when he had had time to succumb to the pressure for "confessions" under prison conditions. These conditions, and those of places to which people were sentenced, varied very much; convict labour in the central areas meant work on construction jobs, and literate convicts were clerks or worked at their own professions. One acquaintance of mine, an army officer who was a Mongol by nationality and offspring of a Household family, stayed on at his convict job as a supplies planner on the Moscow-Volga canal construction after his sentence expired, working a seven hour instead of a ten to twelve hour day and earning 1,000 rubles a month instead of 100 and all found, and of course free to please himself in his own time. We discussed in detail a film of convict life, called *Prisoners*, which was then showing in Moscow, and he said that while in a technical sense it was accurate enough, it completely failed to convey the utter drabness of convict life. Conditions in more distant areas, on mining or construction work, could on the other hand be unrelieved nightmare, especially in camps where habitual criminals and political convicts were mixed, and the criminals ran the camp under an inefficient, cruel or corrupt administration. But perhaps the worst feature was the almost complete impossibility of communicating with a convict, so that families suddenly separated by arrest were, for practical purposes, lost to one another; while another vicious evil was the extension of sentence by the political police authorities. Convict labour conditions became much worse during the war but improved sharply after about 1950— so much so that some foreign prisoners who had been released then could not believe the reports of others released from the same camps two or three years later. The importance of convict labour in the economy is often absurdly exaggerated: for example, J. Scholmer repeatedly says in his book *Vorkuta* (1954) that 50 per cent of the Russian coal output and 80 per cent of the timber are obtained by convict labour. Figures are in fact known only from the annual plan for 1941 (a detailed secret document captured by the Germans during the war and later published by the Americans), in which the N.K.V.D. is responsible for under 3 per cent of the coal and 12 per cent of the timber (this is not identical with convict labour, for the N.K.V.D. has always employed some free labour and has hired out some of the convict labour under its charge; but the importance of convict labour in the economy cannot have been very different and is likely to be less now). The main *economic* importance of the N.K.V.D. has been in the pioneering of harsh new areas.

Even before the war was over, the test of collaboration with the enemy was applied, at a higher pitch of the old intolerance, to the smaller non-Slav peoples of the invaded areas, and sentence was executed by the same instrument, the political police. Four small republics were dissolved and their indigenous populations were transported: these were the Kalmucks (a Mongol people of the Volga), the Crimean Tartars, the Chechen-Ingush of the north Caucasus, and the Germans of the Volga. These Germans, prosperous descendants of peasant settlers in Catherine's reign, thoroughly antagonized by collectivization, had been watched uneasily since Hitler came to power and were transported without awaiting any test. In addition, two smaller peoples of the north Caucasus, the Karachai and the Balkarians, were transported.

Such treatment of whole peoples was a new feature of political life in modern Russia, far surpassing the Russification activities of the Tsarist government; and the same harking back to old evils in a new form appeared in the anti-Semitic feeling which gathered force after the war and came to a head in January 1953, when a number of Jewish doctors were accused of plotting the deaths or disablement of various politicians and military men. The retraction of these accusations three months later began the downfall of the political police as a power in the land; the convict population under their rule began to be greatly reduced by the amnesty of March 1953; their authority was very much diminished by the arrest and conviction of Beria later in the year, and they have now even begun to become an object of public laughter in humorous magazines. One, for example, early in 1954 prints an M.V.D. man's actual report, so illiterate that it is almost untranslateable, but which would be something like this in English:

I orth auth. agent of Surazh dist. dept. M.V.D. jnr. lt. of militia Ulyanov in pressens of foloing witnesses this day condukted destrucsion on the spot where the potteen was brood entirely of the potteen still, troff with iron pipe, one end twisted, lid wich is sercular on top with opening in, by destructing the drink 2 palefuls we finished by spilling on the ground where found sercular and pot, 2 two litres of pottheen and one harfliter drink taken as material evidence and 0.75 litre potheen destructed by tasting with witnesses and with persons prodoocing potheen.

Agent Surazh dist. M.V.D. jr lt.
(signature).
Witnesses
(signatures).

Jnr. Lt. Ulyanov belongs to the body which has been known variously as the Cheka, G.P.U., O.G.P.U., N.K.V.D. and M.V.D. These names are the initial letters of Extraordinary Commission, State Political Administration, Unified State Political Administration, People's Commissariat of Internal Affairs, and Ministry of Internal Affairs respectively. The Cheka stands in people's minds as "the flaming sword of the revolution"; the G.P.U. and O.G.P.U., both based on the house committee system, boasted that they had "a hundred million eyes and ears"; the letters N.K.V.D. mean for every adult Russian the agency which carried out the great purge; when the People's Commissariats became Ministries in 1946 (and the Red Army became the Soviet Army) this marked an age of respectability and settled patriotism in which the political police increasingly and more and more dangerously became an anachronism which did not long survive the scandal of the "doctors' plot".[1]

[1] A warning against allowing a come-back by the political police was published in a literary magazine of wide circulation (*Znamya*) in May 1954, in the form of a fable, as follows:

THE GNAT'S PROMISE

Stars twinkled in the evening sky. The gnats were swarming and biting. One of them was caught. He squealed, moaned, and began to wring his legs. He fell on his knees, in tears, and begged for mercy.

"What do you want of me, citizens? You're making a terrible mistake! You must be taking me for a malarial mosquito—*anopheles*. But do I look like *anopheles*? Can't you see I'm the most ordinary gnat in the world. Just look at my belly! My belly is in a straight line with my legs. But the belly of the malarial mosquito is at an angle with his legs or it even, if you will forgive me, sticks out. And what of the proboscis of the lower jaw? After all, that is the most characteristic feature. My proboscis, as you can see, is shorter than my trunk. But *anopheles*—confound him—has a proboscis *as long as* his trunk. Ask anyone you like, everybody will tell you I'm not telling you lies. Why not look up the encyclopedia, or even Brehm's *Life of Animals*?"

"But," they said to the Gnat, "you bite! Your bites itch unbearably. You make life hell, Mr. Gnat."

"But don't you see that my whole life is devoted solely to efforts not to bite so very painfully? But I give my word not to bite at all as from today. If you like, I'll sign a paper. Have pity on me, miserable gnat that I am, father of a large family."

"A large family?" they ask. "Have you really got a large family? We didn't know that you had a large family."

"You don't believe it," says the Gnat, weeping copiously. "Just take a look at that pool, see how many larvae are floating on it, they're all mine."

They went to make sure. Yes, it was true, more larvae than the eye could see. Maybe a million, maybe more.

During the whole time of the great activity of the political police, three kinds of people have in their own ways understood very well what was going on. The first group were those who understood what was meant by the story of Boris and Gleb, that in all hard or new times there are the cold and wicked men who do the organizing, and the douce and kindly men who bear the cost: and that this is acceptable if the organizing is for the common future. The second group were those who were making their way in the world, and thrusting aside the innocent whose very virtues were obstructing the work to be done. The third group were those for whom the human meaning of the dialectical movement of society gave a context and a universal meaning both to the tale of Boris and Gleb and the contemporary convulsions, and provided a rational criterion of acceptability. For this last group, Marx's generalization that violence is the midwife of new societies was as deeply and painfully true as the tale of Boris and Gleb, and also gave the moral criterion whereby right and wrong violence could be judged. The one group which could not understand was the group that was purged: their battling godlessness was founded on an inability to understand the sanctity of Boris and Gleb, and their enthusiasm for the mere results of Marx's work prevented their use of his method to extract a more general and secular truth from the lives of those saints.

Thus the history of the Russian making-over of Marxism during the Early Soviet Socialist period is only one part of a

---

"Well, after all," they said, "perhaps it's right to try it and let him go, since, in the first place, he really has family responsibilities, and secondly, he is willing to sign a document."

The Gnat became extremely excited.

"Ah," says he, "you don't know how humbly I thank you! May God bless you with health for your kindness, and may all your dear children be generals, Laureates too, and Academicians! I give my solemn pledge not to bite. Some paper please and a fountain pen, I'll sign right now."

The Gnat buzzed, shouted, banged with his extremities on the writing desk, his eyes flashed fire.

They can see that he is a very sincere gnat. They release him, hand him paper and pen.

"Sign!"

And he bites deep, so deep, into somebody's hand.

"You swine, you liar! Catch him!"

Just try to catch him.

history of the making-over of all the systems of ideas current in twentieth-century Russia, and there are few of these systems that have not become the richer for their struggles with one another. The Marxists have become purged of the superstition of worshipping Marx's results; the Orthodox Church has lost its crust of immemorial rustic superstition; Islam has been forced to lose its degrading view of women and has been justified in its doctrine that the land belongs to all. Now that this process of scouring is almost complete, the peoples of Russia possess a very varied legacy of systems of ideas and modes of statement which are clean enough of ancient dirt to be able to encounter one another with respect. To watch the Russian peoples make use of this equipment is one of the pleasures we can anticipate throughout our lifetimes.

CHAPTER VI

HOW MANY GENERATIONS?

THE words "conditions of life" have two meanings: in a poor country they mean the conditions upon which you live, and in a rich country they mean the conditions in which you live. The story of Russia since 1917 has been the story of a movement from the first state of affairs to the second, both as regards the abolition of recurrent famines, and as regards the capacity to beat off invading enemies.

As we have seen, the revolutionary government of 1917 had in prospect three immediately foreseeable stages of political and economic work. The first was the public control of the existing economy, which as things turned out became in a few months public ownership of its "commanding heights". The second foreseen stage was industrialization, in which the Great-Russian working class carried with it by force and persuasion its own peasantry and the peoples of the other nationalities, and transformed both itself and its politicians in the process. The third foreseen stage was the establishment of "socialism", that is, of production by a publicly owned economy and distribution of the available consumer goods according to work done. And all these three stages were intended to be preparatory to a fourth, and furthest foreseeable, stage: "communism", or distribution of the available consumer goods according to needs.

The central question of organizing the country through these foreseen three preliminary stages was to provide a body capable of such organizing work. This was begun by Lenin when he laid the foundation of Bolshevism in 1903, and faced the problem of forging such a party out of the floating individuals and organizations in the Russian working class and socialist movements. Other more loosely organized socialist and Marxist parties competed with the Bolsheviks for the allegiance of the working class and worked among the peasantry:

123

among the latter the most important were the Socialist Revolutionaries, whose left wing joined Lenin's government in 1917 and contributed the agrarian programme of the revolution. During the heroic age, however, these competitors all became, for reasons which varied from the noble to the cowardly, to a greater or lesser degree collaborationist, so that the Bolsheviks were the only party which emerged from that period as the protector against the foreigner, the landowner, the capitalist and the monarchist. The Socialist Revolutionaries were, however, far from having lost all public credit: their name is associated with the Kronstadt mutiny, which brought the romantics of war communism to their senses: to have lost the allegiance of Kronstadt, for whatever reason, showed extreme political incompetence, and the slogan of the rebels—"the soviets without the Bolsheviks"—shows how nearly this incompetence cost that party the leadership of the whole natural working-class movement. During 1921, the still surviving non-Bolshevik parties were worn away; some of their members joined the Bolsheviks, some went abroad or underground, some were put on trial for political crimes such as assassination. The old Russian tradition of political assassination was strong in the non-Marxist revolutionary parties, and went with the high romance of war-communism: the establishment of the "new economic policy" entailed the stamping out of this tradition of political killings.

Thus in fact there has been one political party from 1922 onwards, and from that time the question has been whether, despite the single name, there should be two or more parties in practice. This is not a simple question of party constitution or machinery. Russian theorists say that their country now has two economic classes (the industrial workers and the peasantry) and a "stratum" of administrators, officials, scientists, scholars, teachers, artists and white-collar workers in general. These economic groupings are common to the larger peoples and nationalities. From a narrow point of view, therefore, the three economic groupings and the hundred and fifty peoples each have special and legitimate interests: and if there is only one political party, all these special and legitimate interests must find expression within it, or they will find expression outside it. This consideration alone means that a "monolithic" single party is either an instrument of rule by one interest over all the others, or that all the special interests share, in addition, certain common interests which are the living rock from which the monolith is hewn. In practice, the single party has meant both things, with emphasis shifting from one to the other according to circumstances. The great policy debates of the 1920s show the single party as the forum where special interests meet and either common interests are forged or one interest comes to rule; the party of the 1930s during industrialization shows one interest—that of the modern section of the urban working class—seizing real dominance and "purging" all opponents and rivals; the party of the 1940s during the war and rehabilitation shows the sinking of the special in the common interests; the party of 1950–52 shows the resurgence of special interests and, in 1953, the taming of tendencies dating from the 1930s (and grown rank meantime) by the rise of the special interests of the peasants in alliance with the special interest of all the townsfolk as consumers.

In this continuous and locked interaction within the party, the actual mechanisms of change are several. The most important is political education, which is continual and public to a degree we should find intolerable; its purpose is not only to make the common interests universally known and accepted, but also to make them accepted as overriding all special interests. The second mechanism, at least until now, has been the purging of the party, at irregular intervals, of members of various undesirable kinds: supporters of special interests who pursued their ends without admitting that common interests should override them; supporters of theory in face of the facts; people who became members to get on to the bandwaggon; people who refused the traditional Russian burden of leadership—to imperil their souls as an occupational hazard—and who believed that they had, while in the offices of leadership, the right to choose what among the movements of the led they would condescend to lead; people who were prepared to accommodate short-sightedness and public clamour among the led. All the party cleansings have been publicly directed against people of these kinds, or of kinds more ordinarily undesirable (bribe-takers, etc.), but most especially against the condescending and accommodating. These public statements made at intervals over a generation have built up a criterion below which no doubt many Russian politicians fall, but by which nevertheless they are judged; and any foreign propaganda which hopes to influence the Russian masses must offer either a better criterion, or politicians better than those they have *as judged by that criterion.*

The political virtues opposite to the vices of condescension and accommodation are called *narodnost* and *partiinost* respectively. We have seen in Chapter V that *narodnost* was also a virtue in Tsarist Russia, and that there it could mean several things. This is also the case now. In internal affairs, it means the proper relationship of leader and led; it also means patriotism of the natural popular kind, love of one's own people without hatred or contempt for others but—at least ideally—a capacity of affection for others because of the love you bear to your own. This ideal, first in a socialist movement infested with romantic internationalists, then later in a country of a hundred and fifty peoples, has been and is of the highest importance. The second virtue, *partiinost*, was also born in nineteenth-century Russia, when some of the Household took up the cause of the slaves. In the nature of things, they were very sure on whose side they were, and this sureness was their *partiinost*: they deliberately chose a part of society and stood by it consistently. So also nowadays: *partiinost* is aspired to by the party, and the party may attain it as far as is humanly possible: then the good party man will also be an excellently *partiiny* man. But even in this ideal state of affairs, circumstances will change, and the party may overleap or underestimate the change: then party and *partiinost* will diverge, and the good party man's duty is to bring the party back to *partiinost.* (*Partiinost* means *partia*-ness, and *partia* means both "part" and "party", in nearly all the meanings of the English words (as well as "set", "match", etc.). In political and newspaper Russian, *partiinost* nowadays means the quality of furthering the party's long-term aims.)

These criteria and ideals find the reality of their use at the local level, and every locality at particular times has problems of its own. A list of fourteen White-Russian party members arrested in 1933, for example, comprises seven poets, four writers, a scientist, a critic and a satirist—which reflects the fact that 1917 was for White-Russia also a national revolution expressed mainly in literature. In Kazakhstan on the other hand there was in 1922 a party membership of 20,000; of these, 18,000 bandwaggoners were purged, and even the remaining 2,000 were in no recognizable sense people of a Communist persuasion. Even seven years later in Kazakhstan, the League of the Poor was run mainly by the clan chiefs: and when these chiefs were finally expropriated and their lands divided out, the communist chairman of one dividing-up meeting opened the proceedings by saying: "This dividing-up is not going to be disorderly. Nobody gets any of the chief's land unless the chief is prepared to say that the man has been a good and loyal worker for several years." In other parts of Central Asia, maps of collective farms show that the land was in fact allotted by clans and septs, whether the dividing was done by local people or not. And even throughout the Great-Russian peasantry the traditional unit of life and work was the three-generation household in a village of nearer and remoter relatives: in the collectivization of 1930 the unit within these collective farms was the "link" of a dozen people, belonging to one or a few closely related such households.

So for most people outside the big towns politics and politicians are words which have passed straight from meaning modern economic organization and organizers of a fairly rough sort to meaning public activities and persons judged by criteria which are indeed not ours, but which are not despicable. To people with this background of experience, the suggestion that they would prefer to have two or more parties is either blankly bewildering, or provokes the reflection that one is much more than enough.

Up to the war, it is in general true to say that only in the towns did "politics" mean anything like what we mean by politics; and it is the towns which have produced the single-party political system, partly because of the nature of the factory community and partly because in the decisive industrializing period the modern industrial section of the

urban working class was in fact the indisputable master of
the country. It was for these two reasons that the trade unions
(which included the other sections of the urban working class)
were effectively run by the party members in them; and it was
for these reasons also that there were no mass organizations
of the peasantry parallel to the trade unions of the towns:
there was no force within the peasantry at that time which
could face up to the strength of the modern industrial section
of the working class, or that was growing with anything like
comparable speed. The thrust and drive of this section of the
working class could indeed have overset the whole intended and
foreseen development of the country if attention to political
education had been relaxed, or the content of that education
made more accommodating to the sectional interest. Instead,
it was at the time when that sectional interest was in the full
flush of its victory, that Stalin published a full re-examination of
the philosophical principles of dialectical and historical
materialism as a chapter in a history of the party, written to show
that it was only by sticking to theoretical principle, in situations
that clamoured for condescension and accommodation, that
modern Russia had come into being: and that all the politicians
who had succumbed to these temptations had fallen by the way-
side and left no mark. This history was published especially
for the new "intelligentsia"—the men who had moved from the
benches to the offices: and it gave them new and more thought-
ful fields to conquer.

The sobering effect of meeting the German military
machine was more than offset by victory in the war and the
intoxication of discovering how much easier rehabilitation
was than industrialization itself. The elated cocksureness
was extraordinary; it was often vulgar in its expression,
and always touching in its simplicity. To understand it at
all, we have to remember that it was the first full-scale war
(as distinct from frontier advances) that the Russians had
won in their remembered history: they had expected to hold
and endure, but not to be able to rise and smite. When they did
they wiped out the shame of centuries, and did it thoroughly:
and they came back home in the same mood. Stalin had led
them to victory, and Stalin was the greatest general and greatest

leader ever; the technical superiority of the enemy and of
potential enemies was nonsense, the Russians had the better
machines—and always would have had, if they had had their
rights; as for the pale intellectuals who kowtowed to the West,
or the misguided girls who preferred foreign husbands, that
sort of thing must be stopped; and this sobersided high theoretical talk about objective necessity—where are the fortresses that
cannot be conquered?

The Russian government seems to have been taken aback
by the force of this ebullience, which sprang out of the achievement of practical self-awareness of the working class as a
working class proved to be such by the ease of reconstruction.
This practical knowledge suddenly flooded with realization
all the phrases about the superiority of socialism previously
mouthed by high theory, and was many times multiplied by the
concurrent delight—that the motherland now had sons as
mighty as herself—discovered by the other sections of the population as they joined in with the new working class in ownership of the appropriated, constructed and defended national
allod held now by these three titles of blood and sweat and
free of all alien obligations whatsoever. The government made
no error of condescension; it did not pick and choose what it
would lead, but it was careful in the leadership it gave. The
newspapers and magazines told the stories of great Russian
inventions, but were careful not to overstep the bounds of fact
(though they stretched them somewhat). The intellectuals
were thoroughly taken in hand; but the man deputed to do this,
Zhdanov, had some experience of mental skills, a sense of
standards, a thorough acquaintance with Great-Russian
fine arts, a strong individual personality, and a scent of the
positive side in the current popular demand. The member of the
Politburo who succumbed to the general light-headedness,
Voznesensky of the Planning Committee, was quietly dropped in
1949. The disillusioning onset of the cold war did not destroy
the new-found confidence, but angered it and gave it the edge of
steel which had carried through the heroic age and industrialization, and produced also a touch of bewilderment that dragged
non-condescension over into accommodation of clamour and
found its unprincipled outlet in the doctors' plot. But this came

I

too late in the day: the ferment had produced something greater in another part of society.

The mass of the armies which had won the war were peasants of all the various nationalities. They think more slowly than townsmen; they also had more to think about and more to take in. What had before affected them most closely was their relation to their own townsmen; now they had seen other townsmen and had something with which to compare their own. At the same time, working against and in with the climate, they are less liable to believe in the abolition of objective necessity. In 1950, the job of amalgamating the collective farms into substantial and manageable economies was carried through, and brought the size and scope of the peasant's immediate interests and responsibility up to comparability with that of the townsman. All this leaven was working; and in September 1952 when the Party Congress was a few weeks off, attention was taken from this mostly urban event by two publications.

The first was a serial story by a then almost unknown writer, Valentin Ovechkin, which pulled no punches in showing the townsman party boss at his bullying in the countryside, and contrasting his uncouth ignorance of men with the slow fairness of his peasant-born second in command. This story in itself would have been a political sensation at any time that year; its contrast with the cautious routine of preparing the Party Congress was almost scandalous. As though to show there was nothing accidental about it, a few weeks later Stalin published a booklet of observations on the work of a group of economists, which is interesting in many ways, but had two especial points: he began by a long and elementary exposition of the nature of objective laws in economic development; and, as an illustration of one side of this, told a story of a mistake of some planners who recommended so low a valuation of cotton sold to the state against bread sold by the state to the cotton farmers that the fixing of such a valuation would have meant that the cotton growers would have stopped growing cotton. This booklet of Stalin's was published in twenty million copies; and there can hardly have been a farm in Russia where the story of the cotton and bread did not arouse the deepest thought; while the timing of the publication must have seemed to many that Stalin was going right past the Party Congress and conversing directly with that class in the country which was least represented there.

The peasants took the winter to think things over; some at least of the party leaders, disturbed both by the cold war and the feel of something stirring that might become unmanageable, "discovered" the doctors' plot. In the spring Stalin died, and somebody in high places was nervous and ill-advised enough to appeal to the masses not to indulge in "panic and disarray". This insult (added to the injury of the immediately preceding political campaign against "gormlessness") gave the new forces an edge that they might not otherwise have shown, and events proceeded rapidly. The announcement of a far-reaching amnesty was followed by the retraction of the accusations against the doctors, and by an accusation of irregularities against the political police. In the summer, Beria and six of his senior subordinates were arrested on a treason charge. Soon afterwards, a series of laws changed the whole relationship between the towns and the peasantry to the benefit of the latter. A remarkable feature of these enactments is that almost all the criticisms in Ovechkin's story were met.[1]

These enactments date (as closely as so large a movement can be dated) the overturn from Early to Middle Soviet Socialism, although as we have seen the overturn began to be public in the autumn of 1952, and is of course not completed yet. The heart of the change lies in the fact that the peasantry is now moving into full partnership with the working class; and this has a number of aspects: the greater unitedness of the country as a whole; the greater respect and self-respect of those smaller peoples which are still composed almost wholly of peasants; and in the larger nationalities the greater weight of their country people in the total culture, and the rising into prominence once more of all the traditions and ways of life that were submerged during industrialization, including tolerance of eccentricities and opinions, a more generous approach to real

[1] The continuing instalments during 1953–54 of Ovechkin's story are unprecedented anywhere for their depth, responsibility, clarity and political effectiveness as stage-by-stage chronicles of a revolution by consent.

difficulties of legitimately diverging or conflicting interests, a less superficial and conventional understanding of what is taken to be public propriety in the management of affairs. All this change must not at all be confused with the light-headed and frothy freedoms and romances of the heroic age and the succeeding years, which produced a lunatic fringe of urban culture; what is coming in now is a knowing and quieting country modification of the harsh industrializing way of life; a remembering of older virtues, their knitting together with the newer ones, and the healing of the hurts through which these newer ones were born. Needless to say, just as the onset of industrialization brought destruction to the romantic or gentry-minded revolutionaries, so now those who forged themselves into specialized instruments for the industrializing ways of life and thought are being ousted from responsibility: the heads of the political police were condemned to death; many minor and local politicians have been replaced; and the propagandists and publicists of the unblinking orthodoxy of a past age show their bewilderment and indignation in their writings: they obviously feel that something quite unfair has happened, but have no idea what it 'is. Their helplessness is the surest indication to the outside world that their day is over and will soon be forgotten.[1]

What the great overturn of 1953 means to the outside world is in the first place that no sooner have we come to some judgement of how to live in the same world as Early Soviet Socialism than we are faced with the problem of discovering how to live with Middle Soviet Socialism. One thing we can be sure of to start with: throughout Early Soviet Socialism (including its preparatory period) various other states learned the hard way that it could not be destroyed with the resources at their command; and Middle Soviet Socialism is beyond comparison stronger in material and morale. In the years 1917–52 Russia was

[1]An attempt was made during 1954 to slow down the outburst of the more excitable writings attacking the old hypocrisy, in order to prevent public discussion from running too far ahead of changes in political practices, ideological principles and the standard of living. This attempt is of importance mainly because of the irritation it is causing, an irritation which may in the upshot speed up the whole process of transition. The devotees of the old orthodoxy, however, see it as a sort of come-back for themselves —another instance of their failure to understand what is happening.

hard to treat with partly because she was something new and unknown, and partly because her romantic revolutionary and realist industrializing phases were very different from one another. For example, she had two official and recognized channels of communication with other states and countries: her foreign office and the Communist International. Her foreign office is a perfectly normal institution of its kind, dealing with whales, wives and wars just like any other foreign office; the Communist International was until its dissolution in 1943 supposed to be the channel of communication between the Russian working class and working classes of other countries. In fact, the C.I. often had on its Russian delegation the most romantic and woolly-minded of the Russian revolutionaries who, baulked of scope in Russia, tried to find it outside. They did not, and never could, understand that no working class anywhere would permit itself to be used for their wholly impractical purposes; they traded shamelessly on the respect widely felt for the Russian working class (whom they nominally represented); and when they were nevertheless rejected by all working classes, they blamed their rejectors for stupidity, of all things.

The history of the C.I. is overall a history of failures, some of them appalling (as in China and Germany in the 1930s, but the Chinese communists knew better and their movement survived); and in many countries the only result of its activities was to leave behind a tradition of subservience in the local communist parties to the supposed desires of Moscow which has embarrassed (and been made use of by) the Russians and has infuriated the working classes of other nations.

Since the Second World War it has become much clearer that the Russian working class, so recently industrialized, has various degrees of near relationship to other working classes. The nearest connexions are naturally with those communist-led classes in power in eastern Europe and communist-led but not in power in western Europe—Italy and France. These have, since 1947, a meeting place in the Cominform. The next closest relationship is with those working classes which have industrialization still to come, that is, mainly the Asiatic and colonial in general; and these are becoming the main problem nowadays in world affairs. There is no standing organization which connects them with Russia or China, though various conferences are called from time to time; but in this case organization is internationally less important than example, which will continue to ferment whether there is organization or not. In the immediately foreseeable future, the general tendency in these countries will be that the propertied classes will become more closely attached to the U.S.A., and the property-less classes more well-affected to Russia and China. This presents Britain with the dilemma of choosing in fact—whatever form or forms the choice may take—of handing over our present or erstwhile dependencies (not to mention ourselves) to one side or the other. This dilemma is complicated, in the first place, by the fact that the Russian example ferments far more in our dependencies than in this country; and in the second place by the fact that by sheer weight of wealth Russia and China will together dominate the world in our lifetimes, unless the industrialized countries make their industries more productive. These two facts make nonsense of the two policies so far put forward for Asia, which are (put bluntly) kill them off and buy them off: killing people has never yet stopped the growth of an idea, and buying people is not a constructive policy when the other possible buyer is getting richer all the time.

The largest unknown quantity in world affairs at the present time, from our point of view, is the future political conduct of the communist-governed states, especially Russia. Leaving aside all professions of principle or intentions, there-fore, the question is: can we, looking back on Russia's socialist history, discern trends and causes which we can safely say will operate in the future also? Much of her history to date is specifically the history of an industrialization and that period is now ended: we cannot therefore look for guidance about the future in trends and causes which lay in her industrialization (though we may expect, for example, some of the main features of an industrialization to appear in China in the near future). Some of the characteristics of Russia's Early Socialist period are, in addition to those of industrialization, phenomena which she herself has already done with: the outstanding example is the fluent and irresponsible romanticism of her early socialist years.

Setting these aside, we are left with what are most probably permanent characteristics: her putting of Marxist theory through the mill of native practice; her resilient and resourceful use of Marxist method; the capacities of her peoples for effort and endurance, and their expectation of the same from others; their most laborious procedural proprieties in both internal and external affairs; their simple curiosity and stark incredulity about other ways of life; their determination not to be put upon and their care for their own interests. Their own interests are, primarily, summed up in their question: how many generations are there to be before we can enjoy abundance of materials for the making of our own good life; and secondly (since until then the world is a dangerous place for anyone) how many generations until all peoples enjoy abundance and feel themselves free to make each their own good life? On these questions all Russian policies and conduct, internal and external, are based; and since they are a long-headed and theoretical people, they will continue to subscribe to the ancient view that freedom is knowledge of necessity. Since we and they are not likely to agree in the foreseeable future on the nature of freedom, it is more useful that both should concentrate on the nature of necessity and how it can be known. By this means, perhaps, we can come to understand each other and thereby steer the world through its present dangers into a safer period of its history.

APPENDIX 1

BOOKS

THE following list of books on Russia contains of course only a fraction of those available. I have given particulars of those which give essential information or have, in whatever degree, the gift of understanding. Some axe-grinding books are the only sources available in English of essential information, and these are included with a brief indication of the axe they grind.

GENERAL HISTORIES, NATIONAL HISTORIES, ETC.

G. Vernadsky and M. Karpovich, *A History of Russia*: The first three volumes, which take the story up to the Mongols, appeared by 1953. The standard Western history of Slav Russia.

P. I. Lyashchenko, *History of the National Economy of Russia to 1917* (English translation, 1949): The standard Soviet work.

W. E. D. Allen, *History of the Georgian People* (1932) is the best of the very few full treatments in English of the history of a non-Slav nation in Russia.

H. Desmond Martin, "The Mongol Army" in *Journal of the Asiatic Society* (1943) deals with the military side of Genghiz Khan's unification, and explodes some ancient myths about overwhelming numbers, etc.

Dean Stanley's *History of the Eastern Church* (1861) has not yet been superseded. Other works on the Orthodox Church and Russian religious life are N. Zernov, *Moscow the Third Rome* (1937); G. Fedotov, *Treasury of Russian Spirituality* (1950); and V. Zenkovsky, *A History of Russian Philosophy* (1953).

L. Greenberg, *The Jews in Russia* (vol. I, 1944, vol. II, 1951) and S. Schwarz, *The Jews in the Soviet Union* (1951) together cover the history of a people in Russia which provided many of the better-known romantics amongst the revolutionaries.

O. Caroe, *Soviet Empire* (1954) is the only substantial book on the main Moslem area, but it relies unquestioningly on a very partisan source. Also, it identifies tribal and nomadic freedom with English freedom.

A. M. Pankratova, *History of the U.S.S.R.* (1947) is the school textbook used in Russian secondary schools.

Sir Bernard Pares, *A History of Russia* (1926 and subsequent editions): The best one-volume general history (of the Great-Russians) because Pares keeps trying to go deeper than the record of state events, though he fails completely.

H. Pratt and H. Moore, *Russia: a Short History* (1948): Mostly on the Soviet period; a very useful short introduction, showing an objective insight that has since almost disappeared from American work on Russia.

S. P. Turin, *From Peter the Great to Lenin* (1935): A most useful account of labour conditions and organization, especially in 1905, by a Russian participant with no axe to grind.

L. Weiner, *Russian Literature from the Earliest Times* (two volumes, 1901 and 1903): This is the "Golden Treasury" of Russian literature in English.

P. Bazhov, *The Malachite Casket* (English translation 1942): An old Urals writer relates the miners' legends and historical memories handed down over centuries; the stuff of Russian history as seen by the ordinary people.

RUSSIA SINCE EMANCIPATION

D. Mackenzie Wallace, *Russia* (three editions, 1877, 1905 and 1912): The first book on modern Russia and still the best. Wallace combined to an outstanding degree the Victorian excellences in administration, public affairs and scholarship. His book is a standard by which other books on Russia should be judged.

A. F. Heard, *The Russian Church and Russian Dissent* (1887): Describes the state of affairs in Russian Christianity and quasi-Christianity in the late nineteenth century.

J. Reed, *Ten Days that Shook the World* (1919 and subsequent editions): The classical foreign eye-witness account of the revolution.

E. H. Carr, *The Bolshevik Revolution* 1917–23 (3 vols., 1950–1953): Combines scholarship, lucidity and range. Completion of this fine work and Vernadsky's will at last assemble the known facts, as a groundwork for understanding.

M. Spinka, *The Church and the Russian Revolution* (1927): Remains the best account of the formative stage in the present Russian church, when the breakaway "Living Church" which was encouraged by the Soviet government was decisively rejected.

S. and B. Webb, *Soviet Communism: a New Civilization* (1935): Still the best general survey of Early Soviet Socialism, though the book is really about its authors' hopes for English socialism. But this calm passion gives the book a soul, and the Webbs' scholarship keeps their illusions within bounds.

G. Fisher, *Soviet Opposition to Stalin* (1952): A study of the movement amongst Soviet prisoners in Germany, led by General Vlasov, as units in the German Army to overthrow the communist government. Both the extent and confusion of the movement are shown.

M. Dobb, *Soviet Economic Development Since* 1917 (1948): The author, a Marxist and Cambridge economist, pioneered British study of the Soviet economy before the five-year plans, and this book is a revision and development of his earlier work.

David Granick, *Management of the Industrial firm in the U.S.S.R.* (1954): A study of the works managers in heavy industry during the period 1934–41, which fully uses the information to be found in the Russian industrial press of that period. The author's lack of direct knowledge is evident, but this is nevertheless the best product of American academic studies on the U.S.S.R. in the spheres of economics and of administration. It is an excellent book for the ordinary reader who wishes to make further study of Soviet Russia and who is not worried by footnotes and statistical appendices, which are necessary paraphernalia of academic writings and can be ignored by non-academic readers.

L. Björk, *Wages, Prices and Social Legislation in the Soviet Union* (English translation, 1953): See p. 79.

W. Kolarz, *Russia and her Colonies* (1952) and *The Peoples of the Soviet Far East* (1954): The most useful collections of information on the Soviet government's "nationalities policy", but the author mistakes natterings for analysis.

Y. Delbars, *The Real Stalin* (English translation 1953): M. Delbars is the only biographer of Stalin who knows what politics is. The story he tells, however, is incomplete because he has no interest in economics, Russian history or philosophy, so where these were in fact driving forces in Stalin's work the author replaces them by purely political causes. British readers also have to bear in mind that M. Delbars sees world politics from the French point of view (as for instance in his treatment of Churchill), but this is not, of course, necessarily more erroneous than the British point of view in a book on Russia.

Memoirs of and Visits to Modern Russia

J. Beausobre, *The Woman who could not Die* (1948): The catchpenny title belies the quiet vision and informativeness of this book on prison and labour-camp conditions in peace time.

Count Benckendorf, *Half a Life* (1954): Expresses the best qualities in the final generation of the Russian "Household", and is especially informative about the peasants. This is one of the most responsible and readable books on the Russia of the early twentieth century (it covers the period up to 1923).

J. Davies, *Mission to Moscow* (1942): Diaries, dispatches and letters of the U.S. Ambassador 1936–37.

Eudin and Fisher, *The Life of a Chemist: Memoirs of V. N. Ipatieff* (1946): Excellent on aspects of Russian education, industry and politics from the 1880s to 1930, as seen by a great industrial scientist.

P. Francis, *I Worked in a Soviet Factory* (1939): By a very young Englishman, who was able to get some knowledge of Russian workers.

M. Gordey, *Visa to Moscow* (1952): The most informative recent account of a visit.

J. Littlepage, *In Search of Soviet Gold* (1939): The best personal account of Soviet Russia; covers ten years' practical experience of people in the least travelled areas.

D. Low, *Low's Russian Sketchbook* (1932): Brings the place to life.

T. Matthews, *Russian Child and Russian Wife* (1949): Everyday life from the revolution to the war. The writer's frankness and endurance are more characteristic of Russian women than her values are.

Nikolai Ostrovsky, *How the Steel was Tempered*: The Russian book which most fully expresses the great wave of physical and moral effort and adventure that the revolution brought to so many young Russians. The "steel" is character. The Russians declare, with truth, that each generation of their young people grows up on this book, and the Chinese are now saying the same.

B. Pares, *My Russian Memoirs* (1931): Very useful for the generation up to the revolution. Pares was the grand old man of British academic work on Russia. He had the common touch and understood people well, but as individuals only; he did not understand history.

J. Scott, *Behind the Urals* (1943): A young American's experience over several years of industrialization in the Urals.

M. Seton, *Eisenstein* (1952): Intimate biography of the Russian film innovator, and as such the best account of the artist in the Russian revolution and industrialization.

W. Bedell Smith, *Moscow Mission 1946–49* (1950): An American ambassador's effort to understand Russia. The effort failed, but it had more persistence and weight than the efforts so far made by American scholars.

Budu Svanidze, *My Uncle Joe* (1952): A short record of occasional personal episodes and talks with Stalin over nearly fifty years, freely and responsibly written outside Russia by his nephew. Apart from his own writings, this is the most informative book on Stalin and his ideas.

Vicky, *Meet the Russians* (1953): Sketches of a 1953 visit, with text as perceptive and brief as the drawings.

A. Weissberg, *Conspiracy of Silence* (1952): The best picture of prison (as distinct from labour-camp) life and thought during the great purge, as seen by an intelligent but utterly perplexed foreigner.

RUSSIAN DOCUMENTS IN ENGLISH

The Case of the Anti-Soviet Bloc of Rights and Trotskyists (*verbatim report*) (1938): The function of the trial as a political morality play of great power comes out clearly.

Miesel and Kozera, *Materials for the Study of the Soviet System* (1950): A collection of translations from laws, regulations and policy statements, 1917–50. Browsing in this book is an excellent way of getting a fuller knowledge of the U.S.S.R.

Stalin, *Short History of the Communist Party of the Soviet Union* (*Bolsheviks*) (1938): The most important book of Early Soviet Socialism. Completely neglected by specialists on Russia.

R. Schlesinger, *Changing Attitudes in Soviet Russia: the Family* (1949): Translations of laws, speeches, debates and newspaper items. See also *Periodicals.*

STUDIES OF RUSSIAN DOCUMENTS

Most of our knowledge of present-day Russian life and thought comes from published Russian documents, but the proper study of such documents has not yet begun. A start has been attempted by two rather technical articles:

"A Political Economy of Socialism in the Making" (*Soviet Studies*, April 1953), which discusses one side of the putting of Marxism through the mill during and after industrialization; and "Documents in Study of the U.S.S.R.: September 1952–December 1953" (*Soviet Studies*, April 1954), which analyses the key documents as acts in and records of the whole decisive historical process of that period.

Schools of Writing about Modern Russia

These are in the main three: (1) that which sees the key to Russia as her politicians' appetite for power; (2) the disappointed or outraged socialist; and (3) the psychological school. The most informative of books like these include:

J. N. Hazard, *Law and Social Change in the U.S.S.R.* (1953): The clearest account of Soviet law, illustrated by a large number of actual cases taken from the legal periodicals. The power theory is used as an expository device only.

W. W. Rostow, *The Dynamics of Soviet Society* (1954): The best of several American attempts to discover "what makes Russia tick". All these earnest books see the answer more or less entirely in the Kremlin's desire for power, and their scholarly ham-handedness is painful reading. Churchill said it all in four words a generation ago—"crocodiles with master minds".

A. Barmine, *Memoirs of a Soviet Diplomat* (1938): A refugee who never got over the "heroic age" of the revolution.

A. Ciliga, *The Russian Enigma* (1940): The fascinating experiences and meditations of a foreign romantic revolutionary amongst arrested Russians of his own kind.

L. Trotsky, *The Revolution Betrayed* (1937): An acute, nagging analysis; as informative on why Russia rejected what Trotsky represented as on the Russia examined in the book.

I. Deutscher, *Stalin* (1949) and *The Prophet Armed* (1953): Full-scale biographies of Stalin and Trotsky in the romantical-political-tragical school.

H. J. Berman, *Justice in Russia* (1950): Berman is one of the very few American specialists on Russia who know that people and countries are not machines, but even so the influence of the mechanical "absolute power" theory is evident in his "parental" concept of Soviet law. His view of the Soviet state as parent controlling the citizens as children would be more useful if he realized that children grow up.

APPENDIX 2

PERIODICALS

Soviet Studies (quarterly, edited at the University of Glasgow, Department of Soviet Social and Economic Institutions, price 30s. a year, published by Basil Blackwell, Broad Street, Oxford). Concerned exclusively with the U.S.S.R. in all its aspects. In parts long-winded and heavy going, but its articles, reviews and translations provide the fullest all-round picture of the U.S.S.R. in its present development that is available in any one periodical.

Bulletins on Soviet Economics (prepared and published two or more times a year at the University of Birmingham, Department for the Study of the Economy and Institutions of the U.S.S.R., £1 per annum). A very full statistical bulletin, more concerned with recording than analysing Soviet economic data and regulations.

The Slavonic and East European Review (issued twice yearly by the School of Slavonic and East European Studies, University of London, price £2 per annum). Contains articles, reviews and literary translations on Eastern Europe; covers the history, literature and philology of these countries, as well as articles on the U.S.S.R.

The American Slavic and East European Review (published four times a year by Columbia University Press, price $5.30 per annum outside U.S.A.). The leading American academic journal on the subject, with several articles in each issue on the U.S.S.R.

The Russian Review (quarterly on Russian history and the U.S.S.R., price $6 a year outside U.S.A.). Slighter in size and treatment than the preceding publications.

Current Digest of the Soviet Press (weekly, price $150 a year, issued by The Joint Committee on Slavic Studies, 1745 South State Street, Ann Arbor, Michigan, U.S.A.). Translates in full or part the most important and illuminating current items from about a hundred Soviet newspapers, magazines and learned journals. Worth considering by large libraries which wish to include basic current material on the U.S.S.R.

Central Asian Review (quarterly, price 7s. 6d. per issue, from Central Asian Research Centre, 66B Kings Road, London, S.W.3). A careful and valuable survey of the Soviet local and national press on the five republics of Soviet Central Asia.

The Anglo-Soviet Journal (issued quarterly by the Society for Cultural Relations with the U.S.S.R., 14 Kensington Square, London, W.8, price 10s. a year). Most of its articles, by British and Soviet contributors, are intended to serve friendship between the two countries by pretending that the difficulties in the way of friendship are slight. Also has translations of Soviet articles, and reviews.

Soviet Orbit (weekly, price 1s. per issue, from East Europe Research Bureau, 16 Chester Row, London, S.W.1). Covers all communist countries and movements in a spirit of shocked alarm, and pretends that enmity between Britain and Russia is natural, but does seek to understand.

APPENDIX 3

THE STANDARD OF LIVING

THE standard of living is often taken to mean the same as real wages, i.e. what money earnings can buy, plus free services. This is of course incomplete even for industrial working classes, and cannot be used for peasant populations which eat their own produce, build their own houses and also make some of the other things they need. Estimates of the Russian standard of living are further complicated by the following difficulties: (1) the Russian statistical service, though the largest in the world and the most thorough in the amount of information collected, is not yet expert enough, especially at the lower levels, to provide and collect the figures and to systematize them accurately over so large an area; (2) a more important difficulty for foreign students of Russia is the extremely sparse and selective publication from this great mass of figures, so that a lot of inference and guesswork has to be done to get any arithmetical picture at all. These difficulties are more important to economists and statisticians (whose trade is figures) than to the ordinary people of one country who want to learn more about those of another.

The trade of statistics has its own problems: for example, the Russian figures (which were more fully published up to 1937 than since) can be used to prove either that Russian industrial workers were better off or worse off in 1937 than 1913, according to one's wishes. My closest Russian acquaintance in 1936–37 was quite certain that the food, clothing and housing position was then much worse than when he was a boy before the war (when his father was a platelayer on the railways and the family never went short, according to their own standards). He regarded his boyhood as a golden age of plenty, but at the same time he regarded the revolution and industrialization as a liberation from hopeless poverty, because the country had taken the road to material abundance. He regarded the purge and the coming war or wars as, like the civil war and collectivization, unavoidable jobs of coping with unavoidable obstacles on this road. This man was a party member already well on the way to advancement, but by that time at least a touch of his outlook was becoming quite widespread in the Great-Russian working class. If parents believe that their labour is creating for their children—and perhaps even for themselves—the most rich, educated, secure and happy country in the world, that belief is as much a part of their standard of living as the quantities of meat and sugar they consume. But beliefs are not capable of measurement, though they may be decisive in practical affairs.

It is not possible from outside Russia to judge the strength of this belief now. It is probably much stronger and more widespread than before the war, because the results of industrialization are now beginning to be felt in a fast and steady improvement of everyday life. The widespread knowledge throughout the working class of the figures for coal, steel, power and so forth (with each annual increase now about as large as the total output of twenty-five years ago), is now being matched by knowledge of the percentage price cuts in consumer goods each spring, which is the means by which the first results of industrialization on the material standard of living are being felt.

The average wage of an adult man in Britain would in 1952 buy goods and services up to three times in value what the average wage of an adult Russian male worker would buy. This is about the same proportion as before the war, since when both of the two working classes have improved their standards. The fact that in Britain the improvement has taken place by an increase in the share of the working class in the national income, and is dependent on world conditions, while in Russia the improvement is not dependent on world conditions and is due to a very large increase in the national income, to which there is no visible limit, is in principle clearly known to each working class, and this knowledge is itself important, though not measurable, in the true standards of living.

For figures and methods of comparing the British and

K

Russian working class standards of living see, e.g. an article by Professor Charles Madge of Birmingham in *Soviet Studies*, Vol. IV, No. 3, which compares Birmingham and Moscow working-class families in 1952. Professor Madge reaches the conclusion that a Moscow family with both husband and wife working at average wages had in that year the same material consumption as a typical Birmingham family with only the man working. The Moscow wages assumed in his article are 1,000 rubles a month. But it would be more true to take, for the Russian working-class average, something like 700 rubles a month, and this would change the result obtained in the article from two-to-one to three-to-one as the value of a British worker's earnings compared to a Russian's. The improvements in Russia which began in 1949, when the economy had recovered from the war, were so much accelerated during 1953 that by 1955 the proportion is likely to be nearer two-to-one, while by 1960 the material standards of the Russian working class are quite likely to be the same as the British are now, except for housing.

Most working-class families in the Russian towns occupy a single room (some of them less) with shared kitchen and washing facilities. The amount of construction is more visible to foreign visitors than the increase of town population, and most of the construction outside the capital is industrial, not housing. One of my Russian acquaintances told me that he was getting married and his fiancée had a room, then hastily added in all seriousness that this was not the reason for his choice. Before the war unfinished buildings would sometimes be seized and occupied by their designated inhabitants as soon as they were weather-proof, and so the finishing would never be done. When the lack of housing privacy is overcome, the Russian material standard of living will begin to be appropriate to a modern working class, and one of the worst strains of life there will be ended. (The best information in English on Soviet housing is a series of articles by Dr. Alexander Block in *Soviet Studies*, Vol. III, Nos. 1 and 3, Vol. V, No. 3 and Vol. VI, No. 1.) To a lesser extent, the same is true of shops, which are quite inadequate. Most schools work on a two-shift system and hospitals and the health service are inadequate.

The factory clubs are the main community centres, and they mitigate the wretchedness of housing.

The widespread view that a higher proportion of Russian than British married women go out to work is probably wrong and may be due to Russian propaganda (which regards housewives taking jobs as a good thing, as our propaganda did during the war) and to the fact that Russian women are seen by foreign visitors working at snow-clearing, on building jobs and other outdoor occupations. The occupations employing mostly women, however, such as consumer goods production and distribution, are very much less developed in Russia than Britain. (In the countryside, of course, as in all peasant countries, the women work very hard.) Equality of the sexes is real, so far as this can be ensured by equal pay for equal work and a good deal of help in the form of crèches and kindergartens, but women predominate in the lower-paid occupations. The real position about sex equality was many times summed up to me by Russian women in the statement that it depends on the level of economic development: if you have to fight your way on to trams, spend hours in queues and keep a single room fit for a family to live in, women are handicapped.

The standard of living in any community at any time amounts to (a) the legacy of that generation from its ancestors; (b) what that generation makes of its legacy. It is only the most obvious part of the legacy that can be measured or even described in economic terms. A generation that makes the great effort required to look squarely at its legacy, both the economic and the other sides of it, without complaint, smugness or illusions, and get down to doing the best it can do to pass on the legacy enriched to its own children, has a deep satisfaction that cannot easily be expressed. This satisfaction is most important in the concept of "standard of living", a better name for which would be "fullness of living".

APPENDIX 4

STRIKES

DURING the N.E.P. period strikes were a normal occurrence in the small factories and trading businesses run by Russian private enterprise, and they were not rare occurrences in state-owned industry at that time. But when the first five-year plan started the trade union leaders whose political views were in favour of slow and cautious industrialization and some autonomy for the unions, were replaced from above by others who fully supported the government's policy. In the atmosphere of the plans, any deliberate stoppage of production came to be looked on by the government and its active supporters in the factories as sabotage and treason. Strikes still occurred, but very rarely, and were sometimes avoided by desperate expedients: for example, the manager of a large works in a remote area printed his own paper money for wages when the bank would not provide the cash. (So great is the authority of a works management where the works is the pivot of a town that this money was readily accepted by the workers, but the manager was soon in trouble with the police and his Ministry for forgery.)

There were still strikes in the later 1930s, but there was nothing about them in the newspapers, and their frequency or extent are not known. Some are known to have been successful and unpunished, though it is unlikely that the management and party and trade union leadership in a factory would be allowed by higher authority to continue in their positions in such a case, because a strike would be regarded as a disgrace by the local political authorities, by the Ministry in charge of the factory and by the head office of the trade union. I have no direct knowledge of any strike, though I several times heard that one had occurred. In the Russia of 1936–37 that I knew, the active reactions to a strike by the various authorities concerned would be something along these lines: in the Ministry, dismissal of the manager and urgent easing of the conditions that caused the strike; in the local department of the political police, an investigation of the factory and arrest of the strike leaders for counter-revolutionary propaganda and subversive activities; in the trade union headquarters and the District or Province party offices, a check-up on the influence of their branches in the factory and measures to strengthen this influence through more effective propaganda for the aims of industrialization and through more effective co-operation with or struggle against the management to keep the men satisfied. In relation to a strike, two of the general principles on which industrialization was run would be invoked. The first of these was that any action against production was liable to be subversive, and subversion must be rooted out by arrest or intimidation. The second was expressed in the slogan "there are no bad factories, only bad leaders", and that the responsibility for a bad factory was that of the management and the party and trade union leadership in it, for "it is the duty of leaders to lead", a factory being a community in which proper leadership would make a failure of production due to human agency impossible. That was the theory; the practice must have varied as much as in any other sphere of Russian life.

The situation was much clearer amongst those Russian workers who were employed by capitalist foreigners. Several of the Russian economists and administrators I asked about strikes described with enthusiasm the trade union activities in Northern Sakhalin (the big island off the Soviet Far-eastern coast, north of Japan), which was Russian territory but where the Japanese had treaty rights in the oil and coal deposits. The trade union organizers had a wonderful time there protecting the interests of the workers against capitalist exploitation. There was probably something of the same kind in those places on the mainland where foreign concessions operated, and this extreme trade union keenness was probably one of the reasons why so few of the concessions offered by the Russian government were taken up by foreign firms, and why those that were taken up did not operate satisfactorily to either side.

APPENDIX 5

THE TURNOVER AND CONTROL OF LABOUR

IN the first years of Soviet industrialization the flux of labour was immense. The number of jobs in the building industry in 1932, for example, reached 3,025,000, but in each month of that year the people in nearly a quarter of all these jobs left and were replaced; many of them left the building industry to go into factory work (often in places they had helped to build) or to go back home to the village, and many of those who came into these jobs were fresh from the countryside. Thus the total number of men and women taken on in the building industry in 1932 reached nine millions, and the number who left their jobs was even larger. Almost exactly the same proportion of labour turnover existed in the coal industry in 1930.

Of the numbers who left their jobs, about one in five in such industries as oil, cement, iron and steel, were sacked for persistent absenteeism, lateness, leaving work in the middle of a shift, or other lack of discipline. In the older established industries like textiles, however, both the amount of labour turnover and dismissals for indiscipline were very much lower. Legal powers existed to hold a man to his job in certain circumstances, but were almost never used; on the contrary, factory and mine managers sent out agents to entice individuals and groups away from their existing employment.

During the middle 1930s great efforts were made to reduce labour turnover and absenteeism by improving conditions, fostering skill, and publicity for the high earnings a steady man could make, and by propaganda about the national importance of plan fulfilment. Turnover and absenteeism were still very high (compared with industrialized countries) in the late 1930s, and the following laws were enacted:

20th December, 1938: every employed person to have a Labour Book in which changes of job are noted.

28th December, 1938: official reprimands must be given

150

for being late, leaving early or loafing; three reprimands in one month or four in two months are automatically punished by dismissal. Since people could easily get another job, a new sting is put into dismissal by making the scale of sickness and other benefits, holidays and pensions depend on length of service. This law is given "teeth" by making managers and labour-court judges liable to penalties for not administering it.

27th June, 1940: the seven-hour day is changed to eight hours and the working week of five out of six days is changed back to the normal seven-day week with six working days, making a forty-eight hour week. (Thus Sunday once again becomes the general day of rest.) Labour becomes controlled: a job may be left only with the management's permission, the penalty for infringement being two to four months' imprisonment. Also, the penalty in the law of 28th December, 1938, is changed from dismissal to up to six months' "compulsory labour at place of work". (This is an old Soviet custom: the prisoner carries on his normal work but at less pay, and sleeps in a detention barracks at the works.)

2nd October, 1940: government industrial schools are to be established to train 800,000 to 1,000,000 boys and girls a year aged fourteen to seventeen (these schools produced several million young workers during the war, and are now much better organized than in their early years: they are an important element in the transition from the land to industry).

The main post-war changes in these laws are the dropping of the "lateness" penalties and the direction of labour, which had fallen into abeyance after the invaded areas were put on their feet. These laws were quietly removed from the statute book, without publicity or even any mention in the press. Nowadays labour turnover is still high by our standards, and the emphasis is on big wage and pension bonuses for long and steady service, together with the powerful factor of housing, since nearly all the new housing belongs to the place of work and goes with the job.

APPENDIX 6

THE BANK STEPS IN

THE house journal of the Finance Ministry (*Finansi i Kredit*, May 1953) has a good article on present banking practice entitled "Bank loans and control by the ruble". The following is a shortened translation of a case in which exceptionally severe measures were taken.

A Leningrad soft drinks factory began in 1951 to break the financial rules. Its stocks greatly exceeded the norm and its debts increased. Part of the funds it should have used for production were being illegally used for extensions. The factory did not study its resources. Its bookkeeping reports were always three weeks late. Before acting harshly the local bank did what it could, repeatedly asking the factory's management to make certain improvements, and informing the factory's Ministry of the position, but without result. The bank then, with the permission of its head office, took the most drastic action, stopping all credit, and invoking the law that no supplies for production could now be used until they were paid for. This roused the management to quick and effective action. The accounting department was reorganized so that the current position in relation to plan became clear. Letters were sent to all customers whose payments were overdue, and claims were submitted to State Arbitration. This brought in many hundred of thousands of rubles. The factory brought its raw materials position into more economical relation with its output and got the Industrial Bank to finance its extensions, thus restoring its production funds to their proper purpose. The Ministry did its financial duty to the factory. When after two months the bank restored credit, the factory was able to pay its suppliers and keep straight.

APPENDIX 7

MARX ON RUSSIA

Correspondence of K. Marx and F. Engels with Russian Politicians (published in Russian, Moscow, 1947, 307 pages), includes correspondence over a period of fifty years (1846–95), but is not complete. Marx's earlier correspondence in this volume is mostly with the emigré Russian section of the First International on internal affairs of that organization, and with Danielson who translated Vol. I of *Kapital* into Russian. Danielson writes to Marx in 1872 that the censorship officials have read the translation and advised the authorities as follows: "Although the author is a fully convinced socialist, and his entire book is of a quite definitely socialist character . . . if we bear in mind that the exposition can by no means be called generally accessible and that, on the other hand, the argument is consistently strictly mathematical and scientific in form, the Committee does not find it possible to repress this work and decides to let the book appear." Danielson adds that the censors were mistaken, since the book has had a large and rapid sale, and is warmly praised in all reviews. (The book was subsequently confiscated by the authorities.) The correspondence develops into a discussion of Russian data and problems, especially on whether Russia can by-pass capitalism of the west European type.

Vera Zasulich writes to Marx in 1881: "This question is in my opinion one of life and death, especially for our socialist party. . . . One of two things. Either the village community, freed from the overburdening taxes, payments to the landowners and police bullying, is capable of developing in a socialist direction, that is, of gradually organizing its production and its distribution of products on collectivist principles. In this case the revolutionary socialist has to bend all his efforts to the liberation of the village community and its development. If, on the other hand, the village community is doomed to disappear, then all that a socialist can do, as a socialist, is to work out roughly how many decades it will take for the land of the Russian peasant to get into the hands of the bourgeoisie, how many centuries it will take for capitalism to become as developed in Russia as in western Europe. Then he has to do propaganda only amongst the working class of the towns, who will always be drowned in the masses of peasants thrown by the crumbling village community into the streets of the great towns in search of wages." Zasulich says she and her friends are arguing whether the inevitability of capitalism in Marx's theory applies to Russia.

Marx replied briefly that his theory referred to western Europe, where the private property of peasant ownership had to become the private property of capitalist ownership, whereas Russian peasant property in land is communal. He concludes: "The analysis in *Kapital* does not, consequently, give grounds either for or against the survival value of the Russian village community, but a separate investigation I made from primary sources convinced me that this community is a springboard of social regeneration for Russia, though for it to function as such it must first of all be freed of the destructive influences affecting it from all sides, and then enjoy normal conditions of free development."

Marx dealt with the same point in other correspondence with Russians. He wrote of the village community in a letter to a Russian magazine in 1877: "If Russia continues to pursue the path she has followed since 1861, she will lose the finest chance ever offered by history to a nation, in order to undergo all the fatal vicissitudes of the capitalist régime". He repudiates in this letter those who "metamorphose my historical sketch (in *Kapital*) of the genesis of capitalism in western Europe into a historico-philosophic theory of a general path imposed by fate upon every people, whatever the historical circumstances in which it finds itself"; he illustrates the uselessness of a universal theory which floats free of the facts and compares it to a "universal passport" which gets nobody anywhere. (See, for an English translation of this letter D. Torr, *K. Marx and F. Engels: Correspondence* (1934), pp. 352–5.) Marx took a great deal of trouble over his reply

to Vera Zasulich: he wrote several long drafts for it, but may
have felt, in the end, that the Russians should study their
country themselves, and he sent only the short reply quoted
above.

There are many observations on Russian history in Marx's
writings and notes, and their influence on Russian historians
may be seen in Lyashchenko's book on the economic history
of Russia, which is built up around them. Marx was a great
scholar and studied much Russian material, but his understanding of Russian economic development and ideas is not to
be compared with his mastery of those of western Europe.

APPENDIX 8

FAMILY ORGANIZATION AMONG THE RUSSIAN PEOPLES

By far the longest time of human history has been spent in pre-political societies, but the problem of organization was as chronic then as later. Consequently, just as "state" can mean any kind whatever of political society, so "tribe" means any kind whatever of pre-political societies, and there are probably more kinds of tribes known than there are kinds of states.

When a people reaches the political or state stage of organization it always has behind it a long history of tribal organization, and this history plays some part in shaping the kind of state organization. For example, if the tribe has been large, well organized, and in the habit of adopting members freely, then its political life may be well organized and what we would call democratic or free in general conduct. If the tribe has been hard pressed and disunited, then that people's political life will bear the marks of that experience.

Membership of a state is determined by citizenship, which depends on birth or naturalization; and membership of a tribe is determined by kinship, which depends on birth or adoption. In political societies, membership of a class is determined by economic function and is signalized by marks of social status. In tribal societies, economic differentiation is between tribes or within the tribe between its sub-divisions—clans, lineages, families; between the sexes; between the generations and age-groups: and this differentiation is signalized by marks of social status.

Some of the Russian peoples were still tribal in 1929 and have come into collective farming with their own clan and tribal form of family organizations still intact. There has not yet been time for the effect of their tribal organization on their political organization to become apparent. Some other

Russian peoples passed from a slave economy still strongly marked by tribal organization into collective farming and (to a lesser degree) into industry: in these cases the influence of the clan chiefs and priests over the dependent kinsmen and personal slaves was large during collectivization and often is still. In the Moslem areas, for example, although most of the women and girls now go unveiled, few girls complete the secondary school course; polygamy (although illegal) is still known, even among party members; bride-prices are paid, and marriages are arranged without the bride's knowledge or consent. The principal conflicts between the old and new ways of life in these parts have centred in the discarding of the veil (for which not a few brave women have been murdered by their men-folk), and the payment of labour-day earnings in the collective farms to the women who earn them and not to their husbands or fathers. In this latter conflict, the less supervision there is from Moscow over the local government the more frequently in general have the women earners' rights been infringed in local practice: and the struggle has reached various stages among the various peoples. The overall effect of this old tribal tradition on the new political organization has not yet had time to emerge.

The Slav tribal and family organization has been the most formative among these traditional influences on modern Russian political life. The old heathen Slav tribes, so far as can be made out, were not sub-divided into large clans, but consisted of people of a common way of life in a particular territory, organized in large households of kinsmen dwelling around a common farmyard (*dvor*), and headed by the oldest competent male member of the kindred. In a tribe consisting of such interrelated kindreds, lineages producing notable leading elders within the tribe and within kindreds develop into lineages of rank; and these high-ranking lineages were probably the group from which developed the allodial nobility—"elder" lineages with increasing rights over their "younger brothers". The military government of the Rurikids seems to have begun as the establishment of a special lineage to provide military leaders; the integration of this lineage with the landholding lineages was slow, but is fairly accomplished by 1097, when the

conference of Rurikid princes at Lyubech recognized the
splitting of the Rurikid kindred into a number of territorial
princely houses. The gradual development of the princely
household (*dvor*) and Court (also *dvor*) administration can
be traced thenceforward, and is the source of the Household
(*dvoryane*) of the feudal and chattel-slavery periods.

The internal structure of the old large households of
kinsmen living round the common farmyard does not seem to
have been given a full-scale study with the use of modern
anthropological technique on the evidence available. What
seems to be clear however is that these households were in
practice strongholds of heathenism and ancestor cults, so that
Christianity had even nominally hardly penetrated to the
countryside before the Mongol period. The Mongol policy of
tax-exemption of church lands however soon made the church
one of the largest land-holders in Muscovy, and towards
the end of this period the term *krestyane* (men of the Cross)
comes to be used for peasants on church lands: it later extended
to all peasants and became what it is still, the ordinary Russian
word which we always translate as "peasant". During the
agrarian revolution of the sixteenth century, the average
holding of the peasant household decreased by a half: and
this suggests that at this time the old large household generally
disintegrated into the three-generation household which has
lasted until now, and which is the vehicle of the Slav allodial
tradition.

The study of east-Slav allodial peasant culture and its
derivatives in the noble allodial culture and the interaction of
heathenism and Christianity has been consistently bedevilled
by theories, native and foreign: and while the theories have
changed violently enough, the work has not improved. This
is the more peculiar in that the other modern European culture
with a strong tribal and exceptional feudal background,
England, is very fully studied both here in its homeland and in
Russia itself, whose scholars have produced some notable
work on English mediaeval economic history. It must be
possible to discover why it is that in east-Slav culture the
whole allodial and tribal tradition is concentrated on the land
and its possession (and is now developing into the common

possession of all resources), while in England it has come to be concentrated in personal freedom, so that a slave who sets foot on English soil is by that act made free. This kind of question is the stuff of history, for which all special studies serve, and can serve, only as means.

In spite of the bad state of the subject, however, it is possible to understand a little of how it was that—even in "Holy Russia" —Christianity shaded off through numerous dissenting sects into quasi-Christian bodies which were heathen in all but name, and in the remote areas of the north or Siberia the heathen peasant culture was barely touched. Even in the nineteenth century there were Russian-speaking communities where the presence of a priest at a wedding was not required: the essence of the ceremony was the public feast, in which the attendant population aided the newly wedded pair by homoeopathic magic. Tsarist administration never succeeded in reducing all these forms and ceremonies to a single order even in the Russian-speaking areas; and when the revolutionary government turned its attention to producing a single country-wide family law applicable to Christian, quasi-Christian, Moslem, Buddhist, Jewish and heathen alike, it had to consider the facts together with its own aspirations about the freedom of women. These circumstances, far more than the influence of the urban lunatic fringe, account for the laws of the 'twenties. In brief, these amounted to (1) a definition of monogamy as meaning one spouse at a time; (2) recognition of marriage by repute on an equal legal status with marriage by registration at the Registrar's (religious ceremonies being entirely private matters); (3) the prohibited degrees included only direct ancestors and descendants and sisters or brothers; (4) divorce was not by repute, but registered on application by either party; (5) affiliation orders were made on the mother's evidence alone; (6) abortion was provided as part of the health service on the woman's request.

In the 'thirties the trend of public opinion began to turn (with the formation of the new industrial working class) towards a greater enforcement of family stability: weddings at the Registrar's became more ceremonious; the right to abortion was revoked; divorce became more difficult to obtain.

After the war, this trend became extreme: affiliation orders were abolished and replaced by offering a choice to the mother of keeping her child and receiving a maintenance grant from the state, or of placing the child in a state orphanage from which she could remove it at any time; divorce was made extremely difficult to obtain; and marriages with foreigners were forbidden. This ban was repealed in 1953; and there are also signs that the grounds for divorce are being widened in actual court practice. But, as might be expected in so heterogeneous a population, there is no sign yet of an actual common standard coming into existence: there are peoples among whom intermarriage with other peoples of Russia is in fact almost forbidden (an Armenian family has recently been in the papers for refusing to recognize a Great-Russian daughter-in-law); and some unregistered marriages can still be brought to the court of public opinion for the sake of the woman and her child, for whom the law provides no redress. It is likely that many changes will be made in the marriage and family laws as opinion develops towards the establishment of a single country-wide standard.

APPENDIX 9

"WORLD COMMUNISM"

It is frequently asserted or assumed by journalists and minor politicians that Russia is devoted to the aim of imposing something called communism on the world. This is an error, arising from a confusion of the following:

(1) Marx argued that capitalism had many times multiplied the productivity of labour, but that after a certain stage such multiplication could only be continued if the capitalist mode of organization (*social* production with *sectional* appropriation of the product) was superseded by a mode of *social* production with *social* appropriation of the product. This new mode, according to Marx's forecast, would have two stages: the first stage, in which the socially appropriated product would be distributed according to work done; and the second stage, in which the socially appropriated product would be large enough to be distributed according to needs. Russian communists take for granted as the practical purpose of all their work Marx's definition of the conditions required for the second stage: these are (*a*) ending the tyranny imposed on the individual by specialization of labour, including specialization as a purely manual or purely mental worker; (*b*) reaching a level of civilization at which work is not done as the means for living but as the best thing in life; (*c*) reaching a level of production and culture at which "from each according to his ability, to each according to his needs" can become a reality. In modern Russian thought, the term "socialism" is used for the first stage, "communism" for the second stage, and communist parties are parties which have the second stage as their aim: no country has yet reached this stage; and of all the communist-led countries, only Russia has as yet reached the first stage. Also, in modern Russian thought, all countries now capitalist are bound to come first to socialism and then to communism: but communism is of its very nature not something that can be imposed.

L   161

(2) In the romantic phase of the Russian revolution, this forecast of Marx's (so remote from the poverty of Russia), was taken by the romantics to mean that Russia could not industrialize on her own resources, but must instigate revolution elsewhere (especially in Germany) so that her own industrialization could be parasitic. Since industrialization was undertaken, no responsible body of Russian opinion has held that it is any business of Russia's to instigate revolutions elsewhere. The Russian attempt to set up a Finnish creature "government" in Terijoki during the Soviet-Finnish war of 1939–40 was something completely different: an amateurish instance of familiar Great Power practice in strategic areas, rather ridiculously coloured by the already moribund tradition of world revolution. The experiences of the war with Germany finished off the remnants of world revolutionism, so that when after the war Russia made claims to former Georgian and Armenian territories now in Turkey, the propaganda for the claim was conducted through extremely learned articles by historians (which is a familiar mode of propaganda in all countries), not by international revolutionaries.

(3) The countries in which Russia installed communist governments after the war were all (a) on the Russian side of a line agreed between the Great Powers, and (b) in a political condition inclining to communism. (Finland, though on the Russian side of the line, was not in this political condition, while Greece, though in this condition, was on the other side of the line. The only exception is the Russian zone of Germany, which was not inclining to communism, but where a native communist government was installed as a civilian instrument of the victor's military control.)

(4) This division of the world into spheres of interest is only new in that there are only two such spheres, so that the two sides are coming to comprise the entire world between them. All this is not unnatural as a preliminary to world unification, which requires much testing and sifting of qualities; each of the two sides is like a large umbrella under which a particular set of virtues and vices is being gathered: since there is no independent umpire in history the practical test of competition is the only way in which the sifting can take place,

but the side or country which has the truest understanding of what is going on will transmit the more of its own qualities to the one world. There is no other way in which a country can "impose" anything on the world.

(5) In the industrializing period and afterwards, especially since the war, popular patriotism in Russia has crystallized around first the growth, and recently the reputation, of the state as society's executive. The primary external function of this state, as of all others, is to ensure the security of its peoples and territory; and it now considers revolutions elsewhere in the light of this requirement. For example, Russia in 1947 recommended the Chinese communists not to fight for power, since it feared the Chinese nationalists might prove powerful enough to cause large-scale hostilities which could grow to endanger Russia.

(6) From this present Russian point of view, the very movement of other countries towards the overthrow of their own capitalisms is fraught with dangers to Russia. For example, the threat of a slump, and of a revolution arising from it, may in capitalist economies be avoided temporarily by heavy war expenditure, and Russia may become involved in consequent wars. (Hence the importance of the peace movement.) Heavy war expenditure also at present means great advance in nuclear bombs, guided missiles, etc.: hence the importance of spying (though this has been much less effective than is supposed). But if immediate war is avoided, then the capitalist economies may well become liable to an even larger slump; and the threat or onset of this may produce neo-Fascist governments in the principal capitalist countries. Such developments can, in the Russian view, only be prevented by political education among the capitalist working classes: hence the importance, in Russian eyes, of Russian propaganda to working classes in capitalist countries, for obviously (to the Russian mind) it would be a major historical catastrophe if the emergence of a new socialist country caused or was caused by a war which destroyed or disabled the one socialist country that already exists. The timing and management of socialist revolutions is thus now of more acute interest to the Russians than the mere achievement of such revolutions, which they take unhurriedly for granted.

But the Russian experts on foreign affairs are not well acquainted with the internal affairs of other countries, especially those with old industrialized working classes (for much the same reasons as our experts are not well acquainted with Russian affairs: they are ignorant and therefore credulous): so they tend on the whole to discourage activities of which they are not able to foresee the outcome.

None of this alters the fact that the world is an unsafe place and Russia is a very powerful country whose ways are not our ways, and only a nation without the hope or desire to preserve its independence will reduce its defences below the necessary level. But defence means open eyes as well as weapons. The melodramatic *obsession* of so many of our politicians and journalists with "world communism" (reminiscent of the Russian romantic revolutionaries the other way round) endangers our defences in two ways. It blinds us to powerful or potentially powerful countries other than Russia and to forces other than communism, which threaten both world peace and our national independence. More important in the long run, it blinds us to the real challenge from Russia, which is much more serious than any likelihood of a Russia military attack. This challenge is the new mode of industrial civilization which from the start takes its stand on the intention to create (out of the old cohesion of the society concerned) a new consensus of decencies and disciplines. This need for a nationwide consensus of standards was for a long time lost sight of in the first round of industrialization pioneered by Britain. Recognition of the need is the outstanding characteristic of the second round, pioneered by Russia. Russia's achievement in this respect has been hidden by the great difficulties of her industrialization and has yet to be cleansed of the cruelties and hypocrisies of that process. But this achievement will become very plain during the next decade or two, and there will be a moral and political movement of many nations, not only the backward ones, towards the pattern of virtues now emerging in Russia. The world is likely to become the scene of a moral and political storm in which the virtues of the West may be submerged in the passion for those being built up in the East. In such a situation, what we stand for may go under (which would be equivalent to our extinction as an independent country), unless we begin now to get a fuller understanding of what is going on in the world, so as to make the decisive contribution which we are quite capable of making to the terms on which the world becomes unified.

It is said that when Archimedes grasped the principle of the lever he exclaimed that if he had a fulcrum he could move the world. The two great levers of world movement today, the U.S.A. and the U.S.S.R., may be very destructive unless the world possesses a steady and enduring fulcrum. Britain has a longer experience and deeper knowledge of world affairs than either of these two great levers: we have a tradition of cool and generous judgement and a practised steadfastness of decision. These qualities impose upon us the duty of being the world's fulcrum at the present juncture of its affairs. If there is anywhere in the world where both America and Russia can be understood, it is Britain. We know that the unfamiliar is not less real than the familiar, but this is one of the principal things that both America and Russia have yet to learn. And it is our task not only to interpret these countries to one another but to hold up to each a clean and candid mirror in which they can each get to know themselves better.

APPENDIX 10

THE NATIONS OF RUSSIA

THE *Republics* of the Union of Soviet Socialist Republics are now sixteen in number; they have considerable constitutional rights but are both much more diverse in character and much more under central supervision and control than the forty-eight states of the U.S.A. Among the sixteen Russian republics there are three main kinds:

Eight of them (nos. 1-8 in the list that follows[1]) are small national entities with old and strong national traditions: these are not administered by Provinces but by Districts and Municipalities directly under their own Republic governments.

Seven of them (nos. 9–15) are of old and culturally distinct peoples (two Slav, four Turkic and one Iranian) who lack a recent administrative tradition of their own: these are administered by Provinces (and Cities where these exist) under their own Republic governments.

The largest single Republic is the Russian Soviet Federative Socialist Republic, which embraces the Great-Russian homeland, all the main areas of Great-Russian peasant colonization and the nomad and settled tribal cultures fringing on those lands. In this Republic, the border areas are administered by Marches; the inner Great-Russian areas are administered by Provinces; the minority cultures, according to their size and substance, have the status and offices of an Autonomous Soviet Socialist Republic, an Autonomous Province or a National shire.

1. Georgia.

The Georgian people are formed of a complex of highland

[1]The numbers in this appendix are used instead of names for the smaller places in the map at the end of this book. A capital letter after a number represents an Autonomous Republic within the Republic indicated by the number, and a small letter represents an Autonomous Province or a National Shire.

tribes and clans together with the lowlanders of Imeretia. The tribe of the Meshkians has the longest known history, being one of the destroyers of the Hittite Empire about 1200 B.C. and well known to the Assyrians: they are the Meshech of the Bible (Genesis x, 2). The Georgian kingdom of Kolchis about 750 B.C. is also remembered in the story of the Argonauts and the Golden Fleece; and later the Georgians were in, or on the borders of, the Persian, Hellenistic, Roman, Parthian, Byzantine, Arab, Mongol and Turkish empires. In the eighteenth century the Georgian king Irakli II formed a multinational Caucasian state with an army largely drawn from the highland tribes (including the Khevsurs) and put himself and his peoples under Russian protection as Christians against the Turks. In 1917 there were two simultaneous and mutually hostile revolutions in Georgia (as in the other Caucasian nations), one capitalist and one socialist.

Modern Georgia comprised fifty-eight Districts and four Municipalities in 1950. In addition, the Georgian government is also responsible for supervising the governments of:

The Autonomous Soviet Socialist Republics of

1A. Abkhazia (capital Sukhum: six districts and two municipalities).

1B. Adjaria (capital Batum: four districts and one municipality).

The Autonomous Province of

1a. South Ossetia (capital Stalinir: four districts and one municipality).

The working class consists mainly of manganese and coal miners, and more recently of iron and steel workers.

Capital: Tiflis.   *University:* Tiflis.

2. Azerbaijan.

The Azerbaijanis are a Moslem people who came into existence during the mediaeval building up of the continental trade-circuit. In 1950, Azerbaijan comprised seventy-three Districts, one Municipality and one City. (The difference between a City and a Municipality is that the City has Borough Soviets within it and under the City Soviet.) The Azerbaijani government is also responsible for supervising the governments of:

The Autonomous Soviet Socialist Republic of

2A. **Nakhichevan,** an old free city separated from modern Azerbaijan by Armenian territory.

The Autonomous Province of

2a. **Nagorno-Karabakh** (capital Stepanakert).

The working class consists of an intermingling of many nationalities in the oilfields, and of some engineering and textile workers.

Capital: Baku.   *University:* Baku.

3. Armenia.

The Armenians are now divided between Russia and Turkey, and many of them live scattered throughout the world. They are a very ancient people with a history going back to the kingdom of Ararat in Assyrian times. They claim descent from Togarmah (Genesis x, 3) and are Christians with their own church. Soviet Armenia comprised thirty-eight Districts and two Municipalities in 1950.

The working class consists mainly of copper and other miners.

Capital: Erivan.   *University:* Erivan.

4. Lithuania.

This people moved from tribal to state organization while Russia was under Mongol rule, and absorbed many of the Russian borderlands: at one time Lithuania reached the Black Sea. Later she was absorbed into Poland, and by 1814 was wholly within Russia. As in the Caucasus, so in the Baltic states, there were two mutually hostile revolutions in 1917, but in the Baltic states the capitalist revolution beat the socialist until 1940. In 1950, Lithuania comprised thirty-seven Counties and five Municipalities.

The working class is mainly in lumbering, small engineering and light industry.

Capital: Vilnius.   *Universities:* Vilnius and Kaunas.

5. Latvia.

This people was formed by the common sufferings of its constituent tribes under the Teutonic knights and their various successors. In 1950, Latvia comprised twenty-five Counties and five Municipalities.

The working class is mainly in the docks, lumbering, light industry and chemicals.

Capital: Riga.   *University:* Riga.

6. Estonia.

This people has a history like that of the Latvians. In 1950, Estonia comprised eleven Counties and five Municipalities.

The working class is mainly in the docks, shale-mining and textiles.

Capital: Tallinn.

University: Tartu: the oldest University in Russia: founded by the Swedes in 1632, re-established by the Russians in 1802 but was the centre of Baltic-German culture until de-Prussianized by the Estonians after the First World War; made into a Soviet-type university in 1940 and again after the war.

7. Moldavia.

This people emerged while Russia was under Mongol rule and formed a principality which was for a time part of Turkey in Europe. The Moldavians were divided between Russia and Rumania after 1917 and were reunited in 1945. In 1950, Moldavia comprised sixty Districts and seven Municipalities.

There is not yet enough industry in Moldavia for a working class to have fully formed.

Capital: Kishinev.   *University:* Kishinev
                                        (founded 1946).

8. Karelo-Finland.

There are many Finnish peoples in the U.S.S.R. (and the republic of Finland outside it). Before 1940, Karelo-Finland was an A.S.S.R.; on her enlargement after the Finnish war

she became a Union Republic. She comprised twenty-four
Districts and two Municipalities in 1950.
The working class is in lumbering and the sawmills.
Capital: Petrozavodsk.   *University:* Petrozavodsk.

9. The Ukraine.

Before the Mongol invasion, Kiev was the chief Rus
city; during the Mongol period, the three Russian peoples
became distinct. The Ukraine (Little-Russia) has been under
Lithuanian, Polish and Turkish rule in various parts; and
a group of cossack settlements concluded a formal act of unity
with Muscovy in 1654. The Khanate of Crim Tartary held the
Ukrainian coast of the Black Sea until the eighteenth century
(the last Khan retired to Britain and married an Edinburgh lady);
the descendants of these Crimean Tartars formed an A.S.S.R.
until it was abolished for collaboration with the Nazis. The
Crimean Province was added, in 1954, to the twenty-five
Provinces and two Cities of the Ukraine. With the acquisition
of Ruthenia from Czechoslovakia in 1945, the Ukrainians were
for the first time together under a single government.

The working class comprises, chiefly, coal and iron miners,
iron and steel workers, and workers in heavy engineering,
transport, precision engineering and chemicals. The Ukraine
has much more basic industry than France (which has the same
population), but Great-Russians still form a large proportion
of the workers.
Capital: Kiev.
Universities: Kiev, Kharkov, Dnepropetrovsk, Lvov,
    Odessa, Chernovitsi.

10. White-Russia.

White-Russia has had the same sort of history as the
Ukraine. She comprised twelve Provinces in 1950. The working
class is in lumbering, paper, furniture, matches, textiles and
(recently) engineering assembly plants.
Capital: Minsk.   *University:* Minsk.

11. Uzbekistan.

The Uzbeks are one of the four main Turkic peoples of

Russia, and emerged from old Tartary in the sixteenth century. They comprised nine Provinces and one City in 1950, and are also responsible for:

The Autonomous Soviet Socialist Republic of:

11A. **Karakalpakia** (capital: Nukus).

The working class has a famous cotton industry, and has recently added iron and steel, chemicals, oil and coal.

> *Capital:* Tashkent, the chief Turkic city of Soviet Central Asia.
>
> *Universities:* Tashkent (the Oriental University) and Samarkand. There is also the Central Asian Industrial Institute at Tashkent.

12. **Kazakhstan.**

Another Turkic Republic, of great size, comprising sixteen Provinces and one City in 1950. Extensive agricultural developments are now taking place in previously nomad areas. The working class is establishing the mining of non-ferrous metals, coal, oil, chemicals—all new industries with a very big future and which have in part been pioneered by convict labour.

> *Capital:* Alma-Ata.   *University:* Alma-Ata.

13. **Kirghizia.**

The third Turkic Republic, which contained six Provinces in 1950. The working class consists of some miners, but the mountains of Kirghizia are not yet under full-scale exploitation.

> *Capital:* Frunze.   *University:* Frunze (founded since the war).

14. **Turkmenia.**

The fourth Turkic Republic, comprising four Provinces and one City in 1950. Life is concentrated in the oases in the worst desert in Russia, which however has mineral deposits now being opened up.

> *Capital:* Ashkhabad, devastated by an earthquake in 1951.

15. **Tadjikistan.**

The Tadjiks are the descendants of the Iranian pre-Turkic inhabitants of Central Asia: their history goes back

to the Skyths who brought down the Assyrian Empire, and to
the empires of Persia and Alexander the Great and the
Hellenistic kingdom of Bactria. They were Zoroastrian,
Manichaean, Mazdaean, Buddhist and Christian before they
were Islamized; and their Golden Age was from the tenth
to the thirteenth centuries when their poets, scientists and
philosophers led the world. The long struggle against Mongol
and Turkic conquerors reduced the Tadjiks to a most miserable
state from which they have begun to recover since 1917.
Their Republic had four Provinces in 1950 and their government is also responsible for:
    The Autonomous Province of
15a. **Gorno-Badakhshan** (capital Khorog), the people of
    which are in religion followers of the Aga Khan.
    The working class mines non-ferrous metals and has a silk
industry.
    Capital: Stalinabad.
    University: Stalinabad, founded since the war. In spite
        of its youth, the university seems to possess an out-
        standing man in Professor Bogoyutdinov who is an
        expert on the work of the philosopher and scientist
        Avicenna, and who is building around himself a group of
        colleagues and pupils whose work is as yet without
        parallel among the peoples of the U.S.S.R. It amounts
        to the foundation of a school of eastern humanities
        (history, philosophy and literature) based on the great
        tradition of the philosophers Avicenna, Alfarabi,
        Albiruni, the mathematicians Khujandi and Omar
        Khayyam, Saadi, Navoi, and the religious movements
        of Zoroastrianism, Manichaeism, Mazdaism and the
        Shiah, Sunni and Sufi elements in Islam. The areas of
        Christian tradition in Russia—even Georgia—show no
        signs of a comparable development as yet.

16. **Russia Proper.**
    The Russian Soviet Federative Socialist Republic
(R.S.F.S.R.) is the largest and most complex of the sixteen
Republics. In 1950 it contained two Cities, six Border Marches,

forty-eight Provinces, twelve Autonomous Republics, six Autonomous Provinces and ten National Shires. The capital is Moscow; the Universities are at Moscow, Leningrad, Voronezh, Gorky, Irkutsk, Molotov, Rostov, Saratov, Sverdlovsk, Tomsk and at Kazan in the A.S.S.R. of Tartary. Other famous centres are the Leningrad Polytechnical, the Leningrad Mining Institute, the Bauman Technical Institute at Moscow, the Kirov Industrial Institute at Sverdlovsk, the Kirov Polytechnical at Tomsk, the Herzen Educational Institute at Moscow, the Lenin Educational Institute at Moscow, the Moscow Conservatory, the Moscow medical institutes and law schools, the Timiryazev Agricultural Institute at Moscow. The U.S.S.R. Academy of Sciences at Moscow is the country's chief co-ordinating centre of research and scholarship. (There are now independent Academies of Sciences in most of the Republics.)

The six Marches are: the **Krasnodar** and **Stavropol** Marches towards the Caucasus; the **Altai** March bordering Soviet and non-Soviet Central Asia; the **Krasnoyarsk** March, which covers the Yenesei basin and stretches the whole breadth of the country from Mongolia to the Arctic (the ribbon of Great-Russian population is at its thinnest here, and most of the peoples of this March are of nomad tribal descent); the **Maritime** March on the coast of the Sea of Japan; the **Khabarov** March which contains all the remaining Pacific coastal regions from Manchuria to Alaska, and has four Provinces of its own. One of these was up to February 1954 the Special Area of the Kolyma river basin, a large desolate gold-bearing area inhabited and worked mainly by convict labour and ruled by the M.V.D., but it is now under normal administration.

The twelve *A.S.S.R.* are:

16 A, B, C. The Finnish peoples of the **Marii** (who claim to be the original founders of Moscow), the **Komi** (descendants of the old Biarmians), and the **Mordvinians** who have two mutually unintelligible languages. Komia contains the coal and oilfield of Vorkuta developed by convict labour during and since the war to supply Leningrad by the most northerly railway in the world. There was a great strike of the convict workers there in 1953.

16 D. **Yakutia** covers the whole basin of the river Lena and several other mighty rivers. The Yakuts are famous for their reindeer and their climate: the coldest place in the world is near Verkhoyansk in the middle of Yakutia.

16 E–H. On the middle Volga the Turkic **Chuvashi** are Christian and are descendants of the people of the old Bolgarian Empire. The **Tartars** and **Bashkirs** are Moslem: the Mufti of Bashkirian Ufa is a very important dignitary. The **Udmurts** are Finnish and their clan organization is very strong.

16 J–L. Between the R.S.F.S.R. Marches and the Caucasian Republics are three A.S.S.R. of peoples of the high mountain valleys. The highland clans of the **Ossetians** gave Russian officials much trouble during collectivization, because they persisted in the belief that a (good) collective farm was "our clan" and the (bad) Kulaks were "their clan". The **Kabardinians** first came into the Russian orbit when one of their princesses married Ivan the Terrible. **Daghestan** is said to contain thirty-two nationalities in its population of one million; there are five principal languages amongst them; they are Moslems and "Mountain Jews". Russian has now taken the place of Arabic as the *lingua franca*.

16 M. The **Buryat Mongol** A.S.S.R. is around Lake Baikal. The Buryats are Buddhists and horse-breeders, and their land is now strategically and industrially important.

The six *Autonomous Provinces* are:

16 a. The **Hebrew** in the far east, an undeveloped area which has not attracted many settlers from Russian and Ukrainian Jewry, who are mainly town dwellers.

16 b, c. The **Adigei** in the Krasnodar March (whose capital is the oil town of Maikop) and the **Cherkess** in the Stavropol March: two branches of the Circassians, a people long famous for the beauty of their women.

16 d, e, f. The **Khakass** and the **Tuva** in the Krasnoyarsk March and the **Altai** in the Altai March are Tartar peoples with a proud and lively memory of Genghiz Khan.

The ten *National Shires* are:

16 g, h, j, k, l, m, n. The **Nentsy, Yamalo-Nentsy, Dolgano Nentsy** and **Chukchi** on the Arctic coasts, the **Koryaks** north of Kamchatka and **Evenki** in the Krasnoyarsk March, and the

Khanti-Mansi of the Ob valley are all reindeer-breeding and hunting nomads. The Soviet administration has provided schooling and medical services. The first sedentary Chukchi collective reindeer farm settled down in 1947. The head of the Chukchi National Shire is now a Chukchi graduate of the Leningrad Institute for Peoples of the North, which specializes in training native as well as Russian administrators, ethnographers, linguists, etc. These primitive peoples and Soviet socialism are just beginning to come to terms with one another.

16 o, p. The **Agin Buryats** to the east and the **Ust-Ordin Buryats** to the west of the Buryat Mongol A.S.S.R.

16 q. The Finnish **Perm-Komi** near the Urals are a small branch of the northern Komi.

The fifty or so provinces of Russia Proper are that part of inner Russia which is Great-Russian by majority or by culture: they are the core of the country and have been the base of industrialization and collectivized agriculture.

The above list is of administrative areas only, and therefore does not include the many smaller peoples and tribes whose native governmental organs are village or at most District Soviets, for instance Greek collective farms in the Ukraine, German collective farms in Siberia, Turkic Tepchyaks on the Volga, the Eskimos of the Arctic islands, and so forth. It is probable that all these smaller peoples are now known (many of them were not in 1917); and that their own organizations and names are now understood and more or less properly used. In the old days many even of the larger peoples were known by nicknames instead of their own proper names: for example the Nentsy and other peoples of the Far North were called Samoyeds, a rude Russian nickname meaning people who eat themselves. The discovery and application of the proper names of peoples accounts for many of the changes in names of administrative areas.

Many of the smaller peoples greeted the revolution as it arrived in their parts with a nationalist or quasi-nationalist outburst of feeling. Among the nomadic peoples for instance there was a good deal of talk about recovering the glories of nomadic empires and programmes for the establishment of a new Greater Tartary or Greater Turkestan to rule the agricul-

tural Russians and Chinese. The many Finnish peoples thought
of founding a Greater Finland, and the Nentsy had a programme
of subjugating most of the other peoples they had ever heard of.
The central government has consistently discouraged the
public airing of such views, which were dangerously near to the
preaching of civil war; and because of the existence of these
inflammatory projects has also prevented the formation of
federations within the Union which might easily have become
equally inflammatory—for example the federation of the Turkic
or the Finnish peoples. Such Pan-Turkic, Pan-Finnish and
similar trends were often as powerful within local communist
parties as outside, and the expulsion of party members holding
such views accounts for many of the local purges.

Industrialization has affected the minority cultures in
various ways. The iron outcrops of the Kuzbas were known,
for example, to the native Shorians and after considerable
persuasion revealed by them to the Soviet prospectors. When
the new mines were opened up, the administration spent much
effort in seeing that the Shorians came into the new work
and shared its benefits, with the result that the Shorians were
very soon bilingual and then ceased to regard themselves as
Shorians and became Russians. Thus one of the small peoples
"disappeared", just as small peoples have "disappeared"
throughout history; and the same kind of "disappearance" will
occur among many of the small peoples of Russia, as it has
occurred among all the small peoples whose descendants are
now English, Welsh and Scottish. Such "disappearances" are
of course far from being a bad thing—obviously the Angles
would not have become English, the Picts Scottish, or the
Black Russians Lithuanian if they had not wanted to: a people
that wants to retain its identity can always do so unless it is
physically exterminated, and there is nothing in the world
tougher or more resistant to change than a peasant population.

Another kind of problem arising out of industrialization
is illustrated by the history of the Chuvashi. After 1917 they
lent no ear to dreams of Pan-Turkism, because their history
did not connect them with Genghiz Khan or Turkestan,
but went back much further to the old Bolgarian empire
on the Volga (from which the Bulgars of modern Bulgaria

were emigrants). They wanted to revive the old Bolgarian name: but this was merely another way of expressing inflammatory imperialist aspirations, and the central government would not allow it. The opening up of industry at Izhevsk then became another source of friction: the country Chuvashi disliked the "dirty" town on their doorstep, and the Chuvashi communist party was moved by the same feeling. The government settled that problem by changing the Chuvashi borders to include Izhevsk, which was at the same time made the Chuvashi capital; by this, all the Russian worker-communist party members in Izhevsk industry were transferred into the Chuvashi party, so that the proportion of industrial workers in that party rose from 9 per cent to 40 per cent, that is, it was changed from a peasant to a working class party, and from a more or less exclusively Chuvashi to a mixed Great-Russian and Chuvashi party. This last meant that the Great Russians as well as the Chuvashi had to become to some degree at least bilingual; that is, the principles of "no exploitation" and "no nationalism" laid considerable burdens of work and self-restraint on both sides. When we remember that such changes were being made all over the Union at the time when the working class itself was going through industrialization, we can imagine something of the size of the problem of keeping the peace; and in fact the police were very hot on arresting people for insulting others' race or culture, especially offenders of the more advanced race (who ought to know better). The less advanced people often enjoyed themselves very much in this situation: John Littlepage tells how non-Great-Russians would amuse themselves in a queue by transferring their own lice to their fuming and helpless Great-Russian neighbours. On the other hand, factories in the Ukraine with a Great-Russian labour force have had all their notices, etc., in Ukrainian—a policy which has led to strikes in some places.

Throughout Early Soviet Socialism the organization and administration of industry and industrialization have remained in the hands of the Union government: each industrial Ministry operating in a Republic or Autonomous Republic, etc., has its liaison officer to the Republic government. Thus, in the oilfields of Azerbaijan, where the *working class* is multi-racial

M

and multi-lingual, the *industry* is run by the Union Ministry which has its liaison officer to the Azerbaijan government, the *communist party* is that of Azerbaijan; the local uniformed police are under the Azerbaijan government, the plain-clothes men (for both crime and politics) are under the Union M.V.D.; primary education is in Azerbaijani with minority schooling (including in this case of course the Great-Russian minority in Azerbaijan) according to the numbers of the minority concerned; higher education is the more in Russian the higher it gets. The whole delicately interlocking system is at the same time rapidly developing with a quickly changing situation: and this is why there are so often accusations of "bourgeois nationalism".

The post-war spread of industry into non-industrialized areas is being handled in several different ways. One used in many parts of the world is exemplified in White-Russia, where engineering assembly plants are now established. Another development is new in the U.S.S.R.: the establishment in February 1954 of a Ukrainian Ministry of Iron and Steel. This is the first emergence of local control in a basic industry of such importance. In Kazakhstan on the other hand, where both agriculture and industry are planned to expand greatly in the immediate future, the local Kazakh party leaders have been in February 1954 replaced by high central politicians, in the Kazakh party (not the government) hierarchy. This is in the tradition of central interventions in local establishments: the normal practice is for central party officials to stay for a year or two, train up local people for promotion, and depart for Moscow leaving the new local people in charge. These visitations therefore normally result in a stronger local administration.

The work of running a country with such a heterogeneous population would be complex enough in ordinary times; during Early Soviet Socialism these complexities have been multiplied by industrialization, collectivization, and the war on the one hand, and the necessity of replacing the old Tsarist, Bokharan, etc., traditions of administration on the other. Thus Early Soviet Socialism covers the history of the establishment of a new rule, and within that the dividing out of the functions of organization, administration and government. This history is most easily understood if we take organization (embodied chiefly in the communist party) to include all non-routine ruling activities, administration (embodied in the civil service) to include all routine ruling activities, and government (embodied in the elected Soviets from village to Union) as the place where administration and organization meet. The interlocking of these three functions is embodied in those people who are as individuals members of all three institutions.

The organizing function embodied in the communist party made, and was re-made by, the revolution; government was established during the revolution and reached its present constitutional form in 1936; administration began to be formed on the morrow of the revolution and is still unevenly developed. Up to 1929, rule was mainly through the organizing body, while government and administration were gradually extended to the whole territory but did not affect vast areas of actual life, so that the country ran on a weird combination of revolutionary zeal with the most penetrating and absorbing pursuit of private enterprise. An autobiographical novel confronts these co-existing opposites in a description of the ardent and genuinely selfless young communist lads at work building a railway to open up a benighted peasant area; as they work, the local peasants pass by with their bundles of goods for sale in the local market and jeer at the lads for submitting to such hard labour. The reconstruction period still stands in people's minds for this memory of unremitting and insulted effort in the midst of a vast black market.

Industrialization and collectivization subordinated this black market and gradually canalized and reduced its activities: the changed situation required a new kind of ruling. The place of the old revolutionaries was taken by a new professional organizing group who were Union men rather than members of any one nation or people, though they began their careers in local organization and administration. After proving their worth in such local work they would spend two or three years in Moscow in specialized training in some branch of administration (planning, railways, etc.) and then be sent out to stiffen local administration and organization anywhere in the Union.

The students' hostel where I lived in Moscow was for "students" of this type; its six hundred inhabitants were of thirty-three nationalities. My room-mate was a Great-Russian who had been head of the Agricultural Department of a District in Uzbekistan; before that he had been manager of a Torgsin shop in Leningrad. (A Torgsin was a shop where goods were sold only for gold, jewels or foreign currency, and Nikolai was not to be cheated: he refused to accept any foreign money bearing the likeness of a deceased monarch.) Down the corridor there was another Great-Russian who had been head of a Province Statistical Department's industry section. He was of peasant stock, and his people had belonged to one of the worse landowners of the Household, who (in carrying out the normal landowner's function of marrying off his serfs) had forcibly married the tallest girl on the estate to the shortest lad—these two were the grand-parents of my neighbour. He brought his country way of life into our corridor, where he and his family had two rooms: they used one to live in, and one for sacks of potatoes and other provisions. Another Great-Russian neighbour had been a young communist organizer in the Far North; he told me how once, on a two-day journey by sledge to stamp a member's card, he had lost his gloves but had carried on and was lucky still to have his hands. An Uzbek (with his Tadjik wife and their boy of thirteen) was another neighbour; he had been Minister for Supplies in the Uzbek Republic, Head of the Uzbek planning commission and Deputy Prime Minister of that Republic. His boy spoke Uzbek and Tadjik and was teaching his father Russian grammar; I was helping the lad with his English.

Besides the students there were always visitors at the hostel—people of the same type and standing who dropped in to see old friends while they were in Moscow on business, and who were packed into half-beds or on tables for a night or two. Half of my narrow bed was occupied in this fashion for a few nights by a Deputy Minister of Agriculture from Azerbaijan, who was even more unsophisticated than the statistician down the corridor.

The people at the hostel were all learning the higher flights of planning. They certainly all were able people who knew their jobs and felt they (and everyone else) had unlimited prospects of work and advancement. Most of them were still in their early thirties; they were in Moscow for three years, and at the end of their course were qualified to plan at Province, Republic or Ministry level. Many of them had been campaigners in collectivization; a surprisingly large proportion had fought in the civil war; all of them had had heavy responsibilities, and thrived on them. "We are the masters of our country, fifty thousand of us," said Nikolai one day, obviously far from dismayed at this responsibility.

These were the kind of people who by the later 1930s had become Ministers of Republics or planners of industries. They had come up through organization and government and were now being trained so that they could head the administrative offices of an industrialized country. In 1938 the Planning Academy was re-organized to admit people who had come up through the growing new administration, and consequently students were no longer exclusively party members as they were in my time. But I could not have chosen my time better: I saw the shift from heroism to business, from the making to the managing of a country; in terms of personal careers, from the lower ranks of revolutionary organizing to the higher ranks of administration.

INDEX

A

Accountant
——must obey, but also report, 63
"American technique", example of, 20
American books on Russia, 141
Andrew, plough, 29
——evangelist, 29, 95
Avicenna, philosopher, 82

B

Bandwaggoners, expelled from party, 127
Bank, Industrial, 63
——State, 63
——steps in, 152
Battling Godless, League of, 114
Biarmia, 82, 83
——ancestors of Komians, 173
Blood-feud, ended locally, 114
Bogoyutdinov, Professor, 172
Bolgarian Empire, 174, 176
Boris and Gleb, story of, 99
——story understood, 121
Button, coat sewn on to, 22

C

Communist International, 133
Communist Party
——founded by Lenin, 123
——in Lenin's time, 108
——instead of mob organization, 25
——monolithic, 125
Constitution of 1936, 66
Convict labour, 117
——on strike, 173
Crony, subordinate to works manager, 62

D

Democracy, not argued, 11
"Democratic centralism", 108

Discovering reserves, 64
Dostoievsky on the merchants, 14
——not yet digested, 97

F

Factory Clubs, community centres, 107
——help make housing bearable, 147
——instead of gin palaces, 25

G

Gin Lane, way of life in, 25
Godfearingness, grim, not lacking, 25
Gorky, small engineer from, 56
Gormlessness, campaign against, 131
Grinevetsky, his book, 17
——practical ideas of, 59

H

Heroic age, 19

I

Ivan the Terrible, reign of, 92
——class struggle of, 112
——political theory of, 94

K

Karakorum, first capital, 80
——Papal embassy to, 85
Kerensky, prime minister, 15
Kharkov, an engineer at, 24
Khazaria, Jewish empire, 82
Khevsurs, Stalin son of, 86
——under Irakli II, 167
Knight, gentle parfit, 85
——stabs Russia in back, 115
——Russia's own, 115
Kronstadt, mutiny, 19, 124

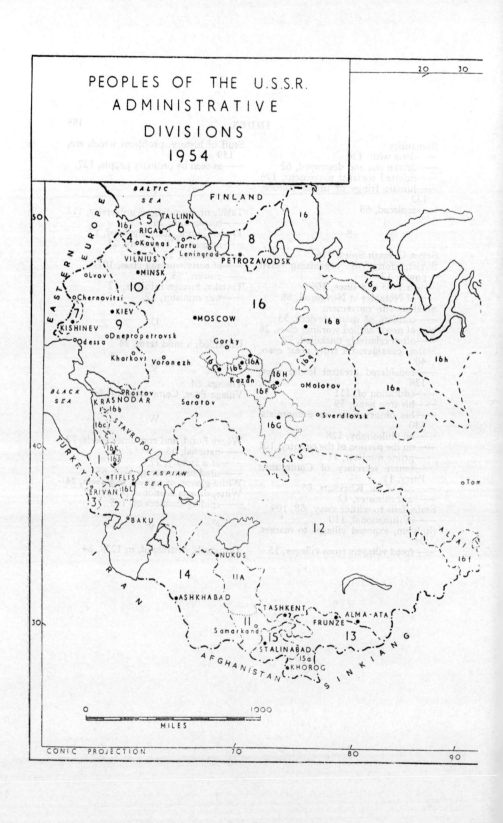

PEOPLES OF THE U.S.S.R.
ADMINISTRATIVE
DIVISIONS
1954

CONIC PROJECTION

MILES

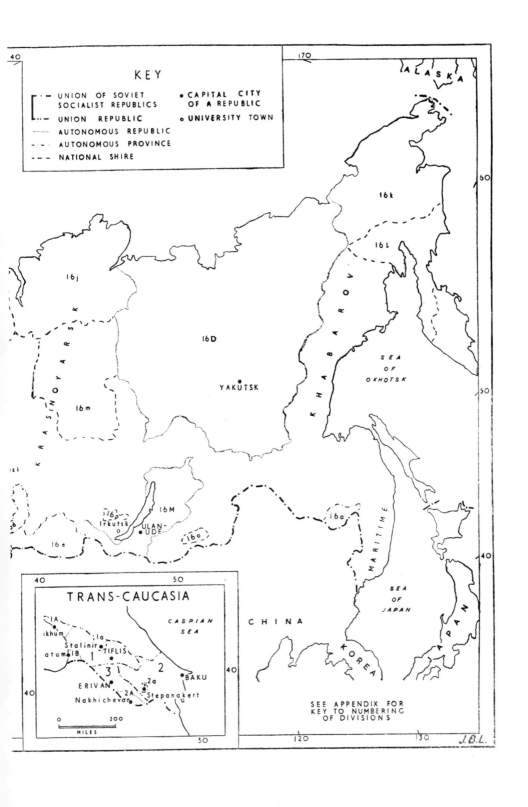

KEY

- UNION OF SOVIET SOCIALIST REPUBLICS
- UNION REPUBLIC
- AUTONOMOUS REPUBLIC
- AUTONOMOUS PROVINCE
- NATIONAL SHIRE
- ● CAPITAL CITY OF A REPUBLIC
- ○ UNIVERSITY TOWN

ALASKA

16k

16l

16j

KHABAROV

16D

YAKUTSK

SEA OF OKHOTSK

KRASNOYARSK

16m

sk

16p
Irkutsk
○

16M

ULAN-
UDE

16o

16e

16a

MARITIME

SEA OF JAPAN

CHINA

KOREA

PAN

TRANS-CAUCASIA

1A

khum

1a

CASPIAN SEA

Stalinir
atum 1B   1
          3   2a
ERIVAN   2A
Nakhichevan

TIFLIS

2

BAKU

Stepanakert

0   200
MILES

SEE APPENDIX FOR
KEY TO NUMBERING
OF DIVISIONS

J.B.L.

For Product Safety Concerns and Information please contact our
EU representative GPSR@taylorandfrancis.com Taylor & Francis
Verlag GmbH, Kaufingerstraße 24, 80331 München, Germany